50 Stir-Fry Recipes for Home

By: Kelly Johnson

Table of Contents

- Chicken and Broccoli Stir-Fry
- Beef and Snow Pea Stir-Fry
- Shrimp Fried Rice Stir-Fry
- Tofu and Vegetable Stir-Fry
- Teriyaki Chicken Stir-Fry
- Pork and Mushroom Stir-Fry
- Cashew Nut and Chicken Stir-Fry
- Sesame Ginger Beef Stir-Fry
- Garlic Shrimp and Asparagus Stir-Fry
- Vegetable Pad Thai Stir-Fry
- Honey Soy Salmon Stir-Fry
- Kung Pao Tofu Stir-Fry
- Orange Chicken Stir-Fry
- Pineapple Teriyaki Pork Stir-Fry
- Szechuan Vegetable Stir-Fry
- Mongolian Chicken Stir-Fry
- Lemon Pepper Shrimp Stir-Fry
- Sweet and Sour Tofu Stir-Fry
- Thai Basil Pork Stir-Fry
- Mediterranean Chicken Stir-Fry
- Ginger Scallion Beef Stir-Fry
- Hoisin Glazed Vegetable Stir-Fry
- Cajun Shrimp and Sausage Stir-Fry
- Black Bean Garlic Chicken Stir-Fry
- Spicy Teriyaki Tofu Stir-Fry
- Lemon Garlic Vegetable Stir-Fry
- Sesame Orange Tofu Stir-Fry
- Coconut Curry Chicken Stir-Fry
- Peanut Noodle Stir-Fry
- Hoisin Pork and Broccoli Stir-Fry
- Five-Spice Shrimp Stir-Fry
- Soy Ginger Mushroom Stir-Fry
- Teriyaki Beef and Mushroom Stir-Fry
- Lemon Honey Chicken Stir-Fry
- Korean BBQ Tofu Stir-Fry

- Garlic Ginger Vegetable Stir-Fry
- Thai Peanut Chicken Stir-Fry
- Honey Sesame Shrimp Stir-Fry
- Broccoli and Tofu in Garlic Sauce Stir-Fry
- General Tso's Cauliflower Stir-Fry
- Sriracha Lime Chicken Stir-Fry
- Honey Ginger Salmon Stir-Fry
- Teriyaki Vegetable Stir-Fry
- Spicy Basil Shrimp Stir-Fry
- Orange Glazed Tofu Stir-Fry
- Mongolian Tofu Stir-Fry
- Soy Chili Beef and Noodle Stir-Fry
- Lemon Herb Chicken Stir-Fry
- Hoisin Eggplant and Tofu Stir-Fry
- Pineapple Fried Quinoa Stir-Fry

Chicken and Broccoli Stir-Fry

Ingredients:

- 1 lb (450g) boneless, skinless chicken breasts, thinly sliced
- 3 cups broccoli florets
- 2 tablespoons vegetable oil
- 3 cloves garlic, minced
- 1 teaspoon fresh ginger, grated
- 1/4 cup soy sauce
- 2 tablespoons oyster sauce
- 1 tablespoon cornstarch
- 1 tablespoon water
- 1 tablespoon sesame oil (optional)
- 2 green onions, chopped (for garnish)
- Cooked white rice (for serving)

Instructions:

Prepare the Sauce:
- In a small bowl, whisk together soy sauce, oyster sauce, cornstarch, water, and sesame oil. Set aside.

Stir-Fry Chicken:
- Heat vegetable oil in a wok or large skillet over medium-high heat. Add sliced chicken and stir-fry until browned and cooked through, about 3-5 minutes. Remove the chicken from the pan and set aside.

Cook Broccoli:
- In the same pan, add a bit more oil if needed. Add minced garlic and grated ginger, sauté for about 30 seconds until fragrant. Add broccoli florets and stir-fry for 3-4 minutes until they are bright green and slightly tender.

Combine Chicken and Broccoli:
- Return the cooked chicken to the pan with the broccoli.

Add Sauce:
- Pour the prepared sauce over the chicken and broccoli. Stir well to coat everything evenly. Cook for an additional 2-3 minutes until the sauce thickens.

Serve:
- Serve the Chicken and Broccoli Stir-Fry over cooked white rice.

Garnish:

- Garnish with chopped green onions for a burst of freshness.

Enjoy:
- Chicken and Broccoli Stir-Fry is ready to be enjoyed. Serve it hot and savor the delicious flavors.

Feel free to customize this recipe by adding other vegetables like bell peppers, carrots, or snap peas. It's a versatile and wholesome dish that's perfect for a quick and tasty weeknight dinner.

Beef and Snow Pea Stir-Fry

Ingredients:

- 1 lb (450g) flank steak, thinly sliced against the grain
- 2 cups snow peas, ends trimmed
- 2 tablespoons vegetable oil
- 3 cloves garlic, minced
- 1 teaspoon fresh ginger, grated
- 1/4 cup soy sauce
- 2 tablespoons oyster sauce
- 1 tablespoon hoisin sauce
- 1 tablespoon cornstarch
- 1 tablespoon water
- 1 tablespoon sesame oil
- 2 green onions, sliced (for garnish)
- Cooked white rice (for serving)

Instructions:

Prepare the Sauce:
- In a small bowl, whisk together soy sauce, oyster sauce, hoisin sauce, cornstarch, water, and sesame oil. Set aside.

Stir-Fry Beef:
- Heat vegetable oil in a wok or large skillet over high heat. Add the sliced beef and stir-fry for 2-3 minutes until browned and cooked to your liking. Remove the beef from the pan and set aside.

Cook Snow Peas:
- In the same pan, add a bit more oil if needed. Add minced garlic and grated ginger, sauté for about 30 seconds until fragrant. Add snow peas and stir-fry for 2-3 minutes until they are bright green and crisp-tender.

Combine Beef and Snow Peas:
- Return the cooked beef to the pan with the snow peas.

Add Sauce:
- Pour the prepared sauce over the beef and snow peas. Stir well to coat everything evenly. Cook for an additional 2-3 minutes until the sauce thickens.

Serve:
- Serve the Beef and Snow Pea Stir-Fry over cooked white rice.

Garnish:

- Garnish with sliced green onions for added freshness.

Enjoy:
- Beef and Snow Pea Stir-Fry is ready to be enjoyed. Serve it hot and savor the delightful combination of flavors and textures.

Feel free to customize this recipe by adding other vegetables or adjusting the level of spiciness to suit your taste. It's a versatile dish that makes for a tasty and satisfying meal.

Shrimp Fried Rice Stir-Fry

Ingredients:

- 2 cups cooked and chilled jasmine rice (best if cooked a day in advance)
- 1 lb (450g) large shrimp, peeled and deveined
- 2 tablespoons vegetable oil
- 3 eggs, lightly beaten
- 1 cup frozen peas and carrots, thawed
- 3 green onions, thinly sliced
- 3 cloves garlic, minced
- 1 tablespoon soy sauce
- 1 tablespoon oyster sauce
- 1 teaspoon sesame oil
- Salt and pepper to taste

Instructions:

Prepare Shrimp:
- Season the shrimp with a pinch of salt and pepper. In a large skillet or wok, heat 1 tablespoon of vegetable oil over medium-high heat. Add the shrimp and cook for 2-3 minutes on each side until they turn pink and opaque. Remove the shrimp from the pan and set aside.

Cook Eggs:
- In the same pan, add the remaining tablespoon of vegetable oil. Pour the beaten eggs into the pan and scramble them until they are just cooked through. Remove the scrambled eggs from the pan and set aside.

Stir-Fry Vegetables:
- In the same pan, add minced garlic, sliced green onions, and the thawed peas and carrots. Stir-fry for 2-3 minutes until the vegetables are heated through.

Add Rice:
- Add the chilled cooked rice to the pan, breaking up any clumps. Stir-fry the rice with the vegetables for 2-3 minutes until it is well-coated and heated.

Combine Shrimp and Eggs:
- Return the cooked shrimp and scrambled eggs to the pan. Stir to combine with the rice and vegetables.

Season with Sauce:

- Pour soy sauce, oyster sauce, and sesame oil over the rice mixture. Stir well to evenly distribute the flavors. Season with additional salt and pepper to taste.

Finish Cooking:
- Continue stir-frying for another 2-3 minutes until everything is well-mixed and heated through.

Serve:
- Serve the Shrimp Fried Rice Stir-Fry hot, garnished with additional sliced green onions if desired.

Enjoy:
- Enjoy this delicious Shrimp Fried Rice Stir-Fry as a complete and satisfying meal.

Feel free to customize the recipe by adding other vegetables or adjusting the seasoning according to your taste preferences. Shrimp Fried Rice Stir-Fry is a quick and flavorful dish that's perfect for a tasty weeknight dinner.

Tofu and Vegetable Stir-Fry

Ingredients:

- 1 block (14 oz) firm tofu, pressed and cubed
- 2 tablespoons soy sauce
- 1 tablespoon cornstarch
- 2 tablespoons vegetable oil, divided
- 3 cups mixed vegetables (broccoli florets, bell peppers, carrots, snap peas, etc.)
- 3 cloves garlic, minced
- 1 tablespoon fresh ginger, grated
- 2 tablespoons hoisin sauce
- 1 tablespoon rice vinegar
- 1 tablespoon sesame oil
- 2 green onions, sliced (for garnish)
- Cooked brown rice or quinoa (for serving)

Instructions:

Prepare Tofu:
- In a bowl, toss the cubed tofu with soy sauce and cornstarch until well coated. Let it marinate for about 15-20 minutes.

Cook Tofu:
- Heat 1 tablespoon of vegetable oil in a large skillet or wok over medium-high heat. Add the marinated tofu cubes and cook until they are golden brown and crispy on all sides. Remove tofu from the pan and set aside.

Stir-Fry Vegetables:
- In the same pan, add the remaining tablespoon of vegetable oil. Add minced garlic and grated ginger, sauté for about 30 seconds until fragrant. Add the mixed vegetables and stir-fry for 4-5 minutes until they are tender-crisp.

Combine Tofu and Vegetables:
- Return the cooked tofu to the pan with the stir-fried vegetables.

Prepare Sauce:
- In a small bowl, whisk together hoisin sauce, rice vinegar, and sesame oil. Pour the sauce over the tofu and vegetables.

Finish Cooking:

- Stir everything well to ensure the tofu and vegetables are coated evenly with the sauce. Cook for an additional 2-3 minutes until everything is heated through.

Garnish and Serve:
- Garnish with sliced green onions and serve the Tofu and Vegetable Stir-Fry over cooked brown rice or quinoa.

Enjoy:
- Enjoy this healthy and flavorful Tofu and Vegetable Stir-Fry as a satisfying meatless meal.

Feel free to experiment with different vegetables and adjust the sauce to your taste. Tofu and Vegetable Stir-Fry is a versatile dish that can be easily customized to suit your preferences.

Teriyaki Chicken Stir-Fry

Ingredients:

- 1 lb (450g) boneless, skinless chicken breasts, thinly sliced
- 2 tablespoons soy sauce
- 2 tablespoons mirin (Japanese sweet rice wine)
- 2 tablespoons sake or dry white wine
- 2 tablespoons brown sugar
- 1 tablespoon sesame oil
- 1 tablespoon cornstarch
- 2 tablespoons vegetable oil, divided
- 3 cups mixed vegetables (bell peppers, broccoli, carrots, snap peas, etc.), sliced
- 3 cloves garlic, minced
- 1 tablespoon fresh ginger, grated
- Cooked white or brown rice (for serving)
- Sesame seeds and green onions (for garnish)

Instructions:

Marinate Chicken:
- In a bowl, combine sliced chicken with soy sauce, mirin, sake (or white wine), brown sugar, sesame oil, and cornstarch. Let it marinate for at least 15-20 minutes.

Stir-Fry Chicken:
- Heat 1 tablespoon of vegetable oil in a wok or large skillet over medium-high heat. Add the marinated chicken and stir-fry until it's cooked through and browned. Remove chicken from the pan and set aside.

Stir-Fry Vegetables:
- In the same pan, add the remaining tablespoon of vegetable oil. Add minced garlic and grated ginger, sauté for about 30 seconds until fragrant. Add the sliced mixed vegetables and stir-fry for 4-5 minutes until they are tender-crisp.

Combine Chicken and Vegetables:
- Return the cooked chicken to the pan with the stir-fried vegetables.

Finish with Teriyaki Sauce:
- Pour any remaining marinade over the chicken and vegetables. Cook for an additional 2-3 minutes until everything is heated through and coated in the teriyaki sauce.

Serve:

- Serve the Teriyaki Chicken Stir-Fry over cooked white or brown rice.

Garnish:
- Garnish with sesame seeds and sliced green onions for added flavor and visual appeal.

Enjoy:
- Enjoy this delicious Teriyaki Chicken Stir-Fry as a satisfying and easy-to-make meal.

Feel free to customize the vegetables and adjust the sweetness or saltiness of the teriyaki sauce to suit your taste. It's a versatile dish that's perfect for a quick and tasty weeknight dinner.

Pork and Mushroom Stir-Fry

Ingredients:

- 1 lb (450g) pork tenderloin or pork loin, thinly sliced
- 8 oz (225g) mushrooms, sliced (button or cremini mushrooms work well)
- 2 tablespoons soy sauce
- 1 tablespoon oyster sauce
- 1 tablespoon hoisin sauce
- 1 tablespoon cornstarch
- 2 tablespoons vegetable oil, divided
- 3 cloves garlic, minced
- 1 tablespoon fresh ginger, grated
- 1 teaspoon sesame oil
- 2 green onions, sliced (for garnish)
- Cooked white or brown rice (for serving)

Instructions:

Prepare Pork:
- In a bowl, combine sliced pork with soy sauce, oyster sauce, hoisin sauce, and cornstarch. Let it marinate for about 15-20 minutes.

Stir-Fry Pork:
- Heat 1 tablespoon of vegetable oil in a wok or large skillet over medium-high heat. Add the marinated pork and stir-fry until it's cooked through and browned. Remove pork from the pan and set aside.

Stir-Fry Mushrooms:
- In the same pan, add the remaining tablespoon of vegetable oil. Add minced garlic and grated ginger, sauté for about 30 seconds until fragrant. Add the sliced mushrooms and stir-fry for 4-5 minutes until they are tender and golden.

Combine Pork and Mushrooms:
- Return the cooked pork to the pan with the stir-fried mushrooms.

Finish with Sesame Oil:
- Drizzle sesame oil over the pork and mushrooms. Stir well to combine and cook for an additional 2-3 minutes until everything is heated through.

Serve:
- Serve the Pork and Mushroom Stir-Fry over cooked white or brown rice.

Garnish:
- Garnish with sliced green onions for added freshness.

Enjoy:
- Enjoy this flavorful Pork and Mushroom Stir-Fry as a satisfying and quick meal.

Feel free to customize the vegetables or add more sauce according to your taste. This versatile stir-fry is perfect for a tasty weeknight dinner.

Cashew Nut and Chicken Stir-Fry

Ingredients:

- 1 lb (450g) boneless, skinless chicken breasts, cut into bite-sized pieces
- 1 cup unsalted cashews
- 2 tablespoons soy sauce
- 1 tablespoon oyster sauce
- 1 tablespoon hoisin sauce
- 1 tablespoon cornstarch
- 2 tablespoons vegetable oil, divided
- 3 cloves garlic, minced
- 1 tablespoon fresh ginger, grated
- 1 red bell pepper, sliced
- 1 cup snap peas, ends trimmed
- 2 green onions, sliced
- Cooked white or brown rice (for serving)

Instructions:

Prepare Chicken:
- In a bowl, combine chicken pieces with soy sauce, oyster sauce, hoisin sauce, and cornstarch. Let it marinate for about 15-20 minutes.

Toast Cashews:
- In a dry wok or large skillet over medium heat, toast the cashews until they are lightly browned and fragrant. Remove from the pan and set aside.

Stir-Fry Chicken:
- Heat 1 tablespoon of vegetable oil in the same wok or skillet over medium-high heat. Add the marinated chicken and stir-fry until it's cooked through and browned. Remove chicken from the pan and set aside.

Stir-Fry Vegetables:
- In the same pan, add the remaining tablespoon of vegetable oil. Add minced garlic and grated ginger, sauté for about 30 seconds until fragrant. Add the sliced red bell pepper and snap peas, stir-fry for 3-4 minutes until they are tender-crisp.

Combine Chicken, Vegetables, and Cashews:
- Return the cooked chicken to the pan with the stir-fried vegetables. Add the toasted cashews.

Finish Cooking:

- Stir everything well to combine and cook for an additional 2-3 minutes until everything is heated through.

Serve:
- Serve the Cashew Nut and Chicken Stir-Fry over cooked white or brown rice.

Garnish:
- Garnish with sliced green onions for added freshness.

Enjoy:
- Enjoy this flavorful and nutty Cashew Nut and Chicken Stir-Fry as a satisfying and quick meal.

Feel free to customize the vegetables or adjust the sauce to your taste. This stir-fry offers a perfect balance of textures and flavors.

Sesame Ginger Beef Stir-Fry

Ingredients:

- 1 lb (450g) flank steak, thinly sliced
- 2 tablespoons soy sauce
- 1 tablespoon oyster sauce
- 1 tablespoon hoisin sauce
- 1 tablespoon sesame oil
- 1 tablespoon cornstarch
- 2 tablespoons vegetable oil, divided
- 3 cloves garlic, minced
- 1 tablespoon fresh ginger, grated
- 1 red bell pepper, thinly sliced
- 1 cup broccoli florets
- 2 tablespoons sesame seeds (optional, for garnish)
- 2 green onions, sliced (for garnish)
- Cooked white or brown rice (for serving)

Instructions:

Prepare Beef:
- In a bowl, combine sliced flank steak with soy sauce, oyster sauce, hoisin sauce, sesame oil, and cornstarch. Let it marinate for about 15-20 minutes.

Stir-Fry Beef:
- Heat 1 tablespoon of vegetable oil in a wok or large skillet over medium-high heat. Add the marinated beef and stir-fry until it's cooked through and browned. Remove beef from the pan and set aside.

Stir-Fry Vegetables:
- In the same pan, add the remaining tablespoon of vegetable oil. Add minced garlic and grated ginger, sauté for about 30 seconds until fragrant. Add the sliced red bell pepper and broccoli florets, stir-fry for 3-4 minutes until they are tender-crisp.

Combine Beef and Vegetables:
- Return the cooked beef to the pan with the stir-fried vegetables.

Finish Cooking:
- Stir everything well to combine and cook for an additional 2-3 minutes until everything is heated through.

Serve:

- Serve the Sesame Ginger Beef Stir-Fry over cooked white or brown rice.

Garnish:
- Garnish with sesame seeds and sliced green onions for added flavor and visual appeal.

Enjoy:
- Enjoy this aromatic Sesame Ginger Beef Stir-Fry as a flavorful and satisfying meal.

Feel free to customize the vegetables or add a bit of heat with red pepper flakes if desired. This stir-fry is a wonderful balance of savory and slightly sweet flavors.

Garlic Shrimp and Asparagus Stir-Fry

Ingredients:

- 1 lb (450g) large shrimp, peeled and deveined
- 1 lb (450g) asparagus, trimmed and cut into 2-inch pieces
- 3 tablespoons soy sauce
- 2 tablespoons oyster sauce
- 1 tablespoon sesame oil
- 1 tablespoon cornstarch
- 2 tablespoons vegetable oil, divided
- 4 cloves garlic, minced
- 1 tablespoon fresh ginger, grated
- Cooked white or brown rice (for serving)
- Sesame seeds and chopped green onions (for garnish)

Instructions:

Prepare Shrimp:
- In a bowl, combine shrimp with soy sauce, oyster sauce, sesame oil, and cornstarch. Let it marinate for about 10-15 minutes.

Stir-Fry Shrimp:
- Heat 1 tablespoon of vegetable oil in a wok or large skillet over medium-high heat. Add the marinated shrimp and stir-fry for 2-3 minutes until they are pink and opaque. Remove shrimp from the pan and set aside.

Stir-Fry Asparagus:
- In the same pan, add the remaining tablespoon of vegetable oil. Add minced garlic and grated ginger, sauté for about 30 seconds until fragrant. Add the asparagus pieces and stir-fry for 4-5 minutes until they are tender-crisp.

Combine Shrimp and Asparagus:
- Return the cooked shrimp to the pan with the stir-fried asparagus.

Finish Cooking:
- Stir everything well to combine and cook for an additional 2-3 minutes until everything is heated through.

Serve:
- Serve the Garlic Shrimp and Asparagus Stir-Fry over cooked white or brown rice.

Garnish:

- Garnish with sesame seeds and chopped green onions for added flavor and visual appeal.

Enjoy:
- Enjoy this quick and flavorful Garlic Shrimp and Asparagus Stir-Fry as a light and satisfying meal.

Feel free to customize this recipe by adding your favorite vegetables or adjusting the seasoning according to your taste. It's a perfect dish for a busy weeknight dinner.

Vegetable Pad Thai Stir-Fry

Ingredients:

- 8 oz (225g) rice noodles
- 2 tablespoons vegetable oil
- 1 cup tofu, cubed
- 2 eggs, lightly beaten
- 1 cup bean sprouts
- 1 cup broccoli florets
- 1 carrot, julienned
- 3 green onions, sliced
- 1/2 cup chopped peanuts
- Lime wedges (for serving)

For the Sauce:

- 3 tablespoons soy sauce
- 2 tablespoons tamarind paste
- 1 tablespoon fish sauce (or soy sauce for a vegetarian version)
- 1 tablespoon brown sugar
- 1 teaspoon chili sauce (adjust to taste)
- 1 clove garlic, minced

Instructions:

Prepare Rice Noodles:
- Cook rice noodles according to package instructions. Drain and set aside.

Prepare Sauce:
- In a small bowl, whisk together soy sauce, tamarind paste, fish sauce (or soy sauce), brown sugar, chili sauce, and minced garlic to make the sauce. Adjust the sweetness and spiciness to your liking.

Stir-Fry Tofu and Eggs:
- Heat 1 tablespoon of vegetable oil in a wok or large skillet over medium-high heat. Add cubed tofu and stir-fry until it's golden brown. Push tofu to one side of the pan and pour the beaten eggs into the other side. Scramble the eggs until cooked, then mix them with the tofu.

Add Vegetables:
- Add broccoli, julienned carrots, and half of the bean sprouts to the wok. Stir-fry for 3-4 minutes until the vegetables are tender-crisp.

Add Noodles and Sauce:
- Add the cooked rice noodles to the wok, followed by the prepared sauce. Toss everything together to coat the noodles and vegetables with the sauce.

Finish Cooking:
- Continue to stir-fry for an additional 2-3 minutes until everything is well-mixed and heated through.

Serve:
- Transfer the Vegetable Pad Thai Stir-Fry to serving plates. Top with sliced green onions, chopped peanuts, and the remaining bean sprouts.

Garnish:
- Garnish with lime wedges on the side for squeezing over the dish.

Enjoy:
- Enjoy this delicious and satisfying Vegetable Pad Thai Stir-Fry as a tasty and vibrant meal.

Feel free to customize the recipe by adding other vegetables or protein of your choice.

It's a versatile dish that can be adapted to suit your preferences.

Honey Soy Salmon Stir-Fry

Ingredients:

- 1 lb (450g) salmon fillets, cut into bite-sized cubes
- 2 tablespoons soy sauce
- 1 tablespoon honey
- 1 tablespoon oyster sauce
- 1 tablespoon sesame oil
- 1 tablespoon cornstarch
- 2 tablespoons vegetable oil, divided
- 3 cloves garlic, minced
- 1 tablespoon fresh ginger, grated
- 1 red bell pepper, sliced
- 1 cup snap peas, ends trimmed
- 2 carrots, julienned
- 2 green onions, sliced
- Sesame seeds (for garnish)
- Cooked white or brown rice (for serving)

Instructions:

Prepare Salmon:
- In a bowl, combine salmon cubes with soy sauce, honey, oyster sauce, sesame oil, and cornstarch. Let it marinate for about 15-20 minutes.

Stir-Fry Salmon:
- Heat 1 tablespoon of vegetable oil in a wok or large skillet over medium-high heat. Add the marinated salmon and stir-fry for 3-4 minutes until the salmon is cooked through and slightly caramelized. Remove salmon from the pan and set aside.

Stir-Fry Vegetables:
- In the same pan, add the remaining tablespoon of vegetable oil. Add minced garlic and grated ginger, sauté for about 30 seconds until fragrant. Add sliced red bell pepper, snap peas, and julienned carrots. Stir-fry for 3-4 minutes until the vegetables are tender-crisp.

Combine Salmon and Vegetables:
- Return the cooked salmon to the pan with the stir-fried vegetables.

Finish Cooking:
- Stir everything well to combine and cook for an additional 2-3 minutes until everything is heated through.

Serve:
- Serve the Honey Soy Salmon Stir-Fry over cooked white or brown rice.

Garnish:
- Garnish with sliced green onions and sprinkle sesame seeds on top.

Enjoy:
- Enjoy this delicious and nutritious Honey Soy Salmon Stir-Fry as a flavorful and satisfying meal.

Feel free to customize the recipe by adding other vegetables or adjusting the sweetness or saltiness of the sauce to your liking. It's a quick and easy dish that's perfect for a healthy weeknight dinner.

Kung Pao Tofu Stir-Fry

Ingredients:

For the Tofu Marinade:

- 1 lb (450g) firm tofu, cubed
- 2 tablespoons soy sauce
- 1 tablespoon rice vinegar
- 1 tablespoon cornstarch

For the Sauce:

- 3 tablespoons soy sauce
- 2 tablespoons rice vinegar
- 1 tablespoon hoisin sauce
- 1 tablespoon chili garlic sauce (adjust to taste)
- 1 tablespoon sesame oil
- 1 tablespoon sugar

For the Stir-Fry:

- 2 tablespoons vegetable oil, divided
- 3 cloves garlic, minced
- 1 tablespoon fresh ginger, grated
- 1 red bell pepper, diced
- 1 green bell pepper, diced
- 1 cup snap peas, ends trimmed
- 1/2 cup unsalted roasted peanuts
- 2 green onions, sliced (for garnish)
- Cooked white or brown rice (for serving)

Instructions:

Prepare Tofu:
- In a bowl, combine tofu cubes with soy sauce, rice vinegar, and cornstarch. Let it marinate for about 15-20 minutes.

Prepare Sauce:
- In another bowl, whisk together soy sauce, rice vinegar, hoisin sauce, chili garlic sauce, sesame oil, and sugar to make the sauce.

Stir-Fry Tofu:

- Heat 1 tablespoon of vegetable oil in a wok or large skillet over medium-high heat. Add the marinated tofu and stir-fry for 4-5 minutes until golden and slightly crispy. Remove tofu from the pan and set aside.

Stir-Fry Vegetables:
- In the same pan, add the remaining tablespoon of vegetable oil. Add minced garlic and grated ginger, sauté for about 30 seconds until fragrant. Add diced red and green bell peppers and snap peas. Stir-fry for 3-4 minutes until the vegetables are tender-crisp.

Combine Tofu and Vegetables:
- Return the cooked tofu to the pan with the stir-fried vegetables.

Add Sauce and Peanuts:
- Pour the prepared sauce over the tofu and vegetables. Add roasted peanuts. Stir everything well to combine.

Finish Cooking:
- Continue to stir-fry for an additional 2-3 minutes until everything is well-coated and heated through.

Serve:
- Serve the Kung Pao Tofu Stir-Fry over cooked white or brown rice.

Garnish:
- Garnish with sliced green onions on top.

Enjoy:
- Enjoy this flavorful and spicy Kung Pao Tofu Stir-Fry as a satisfying and meatless meal.

Feel free to adjust the level of spiciness according to your preference and customize the vegetables to suit your taste. It's a delicious and hearty vegetarian stir-fry.

Orange Chicken Stir-Fry

Ingredients:

For the Chicken Marinade:

- 1 lb (450g) boneless, skinless chicken breasts, cut into bite-sized pieces
- 2 tablespoons soy sauce
- 1 tablespoon rice vinegar
- 1 tablespoon cornstarch

For the Orange Sauce:

- 1/2 cup orange juice (freshly squeezed)
- 2 tablespoons soy sauce
- 2 tablespoons honey
- 1 tablespoon rice vinegar
- 1 teaspoon sesame oil
- 1 teaspoon cornstarch

For the Stir-Fry:

- 2 tablespoons vegetable oil, divided
- 3 cloves garlic, minced
- 1 tablespoon fresh ginger, grated
- 1 orange, zest and segments
- 1 red bell pepper, sliced
- 1 cup snap peas, ends trimmed
- Cooked white or brown rice (for serving)
- Sesame seeds and sliced green onions (for garnish)

Instructions:

Marinate Chicken:
- In a bowl, combine chicken pieces with soy sauce, rice vinegar, and cornstarch. Let it marinate for about 15-20 minutes.

Prepare Orange Sauce:
- In another bowl, whisk together orange juice, soy sauce, honey, rice vinegar, sesame oil, and cornstarch to make the sauce.

Stir-Fry Chicken:
- Heat 1 tablespoon of vegetable oil in a wok or large skillet over medium-high heat. Add the marinated chicken and stir-fry for 4-5 minutes

until it's cooked through and slightly browned. Remove chicken from the pan and set aside.

Stir-Fry Vegetables:
- In the same pan, add the remaining tablespoon of vegetable oil. Add minced garlic and grated ginger, sauté for about 30 seconds until fragrant. Add sliced red bell pepper and snap peas, stir-fry for 3-4 minutes until they are tender-crisp.

Combine Chicken and Vegetables:
- Return the cooked chicken to the pan with the stir-fried vegetables.

Add Orange Zest and Segments:
- Add the zest of one orange and the segmented orange pieces to the pan. Stir well to combine.

Pour Orange Sauce:
- Pour the prepared orange sauce over the chicken and vegetables. Stir everything together.

Finish Cooking:
- Continue to stir-fry for an additional 2-3 minutes until everything is well-coated and heated through.

Serve:
- Serve the Orange Chicken Stir-Fry over cooked white or brown rice.

Garnish:
- Garnish with sesame seeds and sliced green onions on top.

Enjoy:
- Enjoy this flavorful and citrusy Orange Chicken Stir-Fry as a delicious and vibrant meal.

Feel free to customize the recipe by adding more vegetables or adjusting the sweetness and tanginess of the sauce to your liking. It's a quick and tasty stir-fry that's perfect for a weeknight dinner.

Pineapple Teriyaki Pork Stir-Fry

Ingredients:

For the Pork Marinade:

- 1 lb (450g) pork tenderloin, thinly sliced
- 2 tablespoons soy sauce
- 1 tablespoon rice vinegar
- 1 tablespoon cornstarch

For the Teriyaki Sauce:

- 1/4 cup soy sauce
- 2 tablespoons honey
- 1 tablespoon rice vinegar
- 1 teaspoon sesame oil
- 1 teaspoon cornstarch
- 1/2 cup pineapple juice (from canned pineapple chunks)

For the Stir-Fry:

- 2 tablespoons vegetable oil, divided
- 3 cloves garlic, minced
- 1 tablespoon fresh ginger, grated
- 1 red bell pepper, sliced
- 1 cup pineapple chunks (fresh or canned)
- 1 cup snap peas, ends trimmed
- Cooked white or brown rice (for serving)
- Sesame seeds and sliced green onions (for garnish)

Instructions:

Marinate Pork:
- In a bowl, combine sliced pork with soy sauce, rice vinegar, and cornstarch. Let it marinate for about 15-20 minutes.

Prepare Teriyaki Sauce:
- In another bowl, whisk together soy sauce, honey, rice vinegar, sesame oil, cornstarch, and pineapple juice to make the teriyaki sauce.

Stir-Fry Pork:
- Heat 1 tablespoon of vegetable oil in a wok or large skillet over medium-high heat. Add the marinated pork and stir-fry for 4-5 minutes

until it's cooked through and slightly browned. Remove pork from the pan and set aside.

Stir-Fry Vegetables and Pineapple:
- In the same pan, add the remaining tablespoon of vegetable oil. Add minced garlic and grated ginger, sauté for about 30 seconds until fragrant. Add sliced red bell pepper, pineapple chunks, and snap peas. Stir-fry for 3-4 minutes until the vegetables are tender-crisp.

Combine Pork and Vegetables:
- Return the cooked pork to the pan with the stir-fried vegetables and pineapple.

Pour Teriyaki Sauce:
- Pour the prepared teriyaki sauce over the pork and vegetables. Stir everything together.

Finish Cooking:
- Continue to stir-fry for an additional 2-3 minutes until everything is well-coated and heated through.

Serve:
- Serve the Pineapple Teriyaki Pork Stir-Fry over cooked white or brown rice.

Garnish:
- Garnish with sesame seeds and sliced green onions on top.

Enjoy:
- Enjoy this delicious and tropical Pineapple Teriyaki Pork Stir-Fry as a flavorful and satisfying meal.

Feel free to customize the recipe by adding more vegetables or adjusting the sweetness and saltiness of the sauce to your liking. It's a perfect combination of sweet and savory flavors.

Szechuan Vegetable Stir-Fry

Ingredients:

For the Stir-Fry Sauce:

- 3 tablespoons soy sauce
- 2 tablespoons rice vinegar
- 1 tablespoon hoisin sauce
- 1 tablespoon sesame oil
- 1 tablespoon sugar
- 1 teaspoon cornstarch
- 1 teaspoon Szechuan peppercorns, crushed (adjust to taste for spiciness)

For the Stir-Fry:

- 2 tablespoons vegetable oil
- 3 cloves garlic, minced
- 1 tablespoon fresh ginger, grated
- 1 red bell pepper, sliced
- 1 yellow bell pepper, sliced
- 1 cup broccoli florets
- 1 carrot, julienned
- 1 zucchini, sliced
- 1 cup snap peas, ends trimmed
- 1 cup baby corn, halved
- 2 green onions, sliced (for garnish)
- Cooked white or brown rice (for serving)

Instructions:

Prepare Stir-Fry Sauce:
- In a bowl, whisk together soy sauce, rice vinegar, hoisin sauce, sesame oil, sugar, cornstarch, and crushed Szechuan peppercorns. Set aside.

Stir-Fry Vegetables:
- Heat vegetable oil in a wok or large skillet over medium-high heat. Add minced garlic and grated ginger, sauté for about 30 seconds until fragrant. Add sliced red and yellow bell peppers, broccoli florets, julienned carrot, sliced zucchini, snap peas, and baby corn. Stir-fry for 4-5 minutes until the vegetables are tender-crisp.

Add Stir-Fry Sauce:
- Pour the prepared stir-fry sauce over the vegetables. Stir everything well to coat the vegetables evenly.

Finish Cooking:
- Continue to stir-fry for an additional 2-3 minutes until the sauce thickens and coats the vegetables.

Serve:
- Serve the Szechuan Vegetable Stir-Fry over cooked white or brown rice.

Garnish:
- Garnish with sliced green onions on top.

Enjoy:
- Enjoy this spicy and flavorful Szechuan Vegetable Stir-Fry as a delicious and vibrant meal.

Feel free to customize the recipe by adding your favorite vegetables or adjusting the level of spiciness to suit your taste. It's a quick and satisfying stir-fry that brings bold flavors to your table.

Mongolian Chicken Stir-Fry

Ingredients:

For the Chicken Marinade:

- 1 lb (450g) boneless, skinless chicken thighs, thinly sliced
- 2 tablespoons soy sauce
- 1 tablespoon cornstarch

For the Stir-Fry Sauce:

- 1/2 cup soy sauce
- 1/4 cup hoisin sauce
- 2 tablespoons oyster sauce
- 2 tablespoons brown sugar
- 1 tablespoon rice vinegar
- 1 teaspoon sesame oil

For the Stir-Fry:

- 2 tablespoons vegetable oil
- 3 cloves garlic, minced
- 1 tablespoon fresh ginger, grated
- 1 bunch green onions, sliced (white and green parts separated)
- Sesame seeds (for garnish)
- Cooked white or brown rice (for serving)

Instructions:

Marinate Chicken:
- In a bowl, combine sliced chicken with soy sauce and cornstarch. Let it marinate for about 15-20 minutes.

Prepare Stir-Fry Sauce:
- In another bowl, whisk together soy sauce, hoisin sauce, oyster sauce, brown sugar, rice vinegar, and sesame oil to make the sauce.

Stir-Fry Chicken:
- Heat vegetable oil in a wok or large skillet over medium-high heat. Add marinated chicken and stir-fry for 4-5 minutes until cooked through and browned. Remove chicken from the pan and set aside.

Stir-Fry Aromatics:

- In the same pan, add a bit more oil if needed. Add minced garlic, grated ginger, and the white parts of the sliced green onions. Sauté for about 30 seconds until fragrant.

Combine Chicken and Sauce:

- Return the cooked chicken to the pan with the aromatics. Pour the prepared stir-fry sauce over the chicken. Stir everything well to coat the chicken in the sauce.

Finish Cooking:

- Continue to stir-fry for an additional 2-3 minutes until the sauce thickens and coats the chicken.

Serve:

- Serve the Mongolian Chicken Stir-Fry over cooked white or brown rice.

Garnish:

- Garnish with the remaining green parts of the sliced green onions and sprinkle sesame seeds on top.

Enjoy:

- Enjoy this delicious and savory Mongolian Chicken Stir-Fry as a quick and flavorful meal.

Feel free to customize the recipe by adding vegetables like bell peppers or broccoli. The sauce's combination of savory and sweet flavors makes this dish a favorite for stir-fry enthusiasts.

Lemon Pepper Shrimp Stir-Fry

Ingredients:

- 1 lb (450g) large shrimp, peeled and deveined
- 2 tablespoons vegetable oil
- 3 cloves garlic, minced
- 1 tablespoon fresh ginger, grated
- 1 red bell pepper, thinly sliced
- 1 yellow bell pepper, thinly sliced
- 1 cup snow peas, ends trimmed
- 1 lemon, zest and juice
- 1 tablespoon soy sauce
- 1 teaspoon black pepper (adjust to taste)
- 1 tablespoon cornstarch
- 2 tablespoons water
- 2 green onions, sliced (for garnish)
- Cooked white or brown rice (for serving)

Instructions:

Prepare Shrimp:
- Pat the shrimp dry with paper towels. In a bowl, toss the shrimp with soy sauce, black pepper, and cornstarch. Set aside.

Stir-Fry Shrimp:
- Heat vegetable oil in a wok or large skillet over medium-high heat. Add minced garlic and grated ginger, sauté for about 30 seconds until fragrant. Add the marinated shrimp and stir-fry for 2-3 minutes until they are pink and opaque. Remove shrimp from the pan and set aside.

Stir-Fry Vegetables:
- In the same pan, add a bit more oil if needed. Add sliced red and yellow bell peppers and snow peas. Stir-fry for 3-4 minutes until the vegetables are tender-crisp.

Combine Shrimp and Vegetables:
- Return the cooked shrimp to the pan with the stir-fried vegetables.

Add Lemon Zest and Juice:
- Add the zest of one lemon and the juice of the same lemon to the pan. Stir well to combine.

Finish Cooking:

- Continue to stir-fry for an additional 1-2 minutes until everything is heated through and well-coated in the lemon pepper sauce.

Serve:
- Serve the Lemon Pepper Shrimp Stir-Fry over cooked white or brown rice.

Garnish:
- Garnish with sliced green onions on top.

Enjoy:
- Enjoy this zesty and flavorful Lemon Pepper Shrimp Stir-Fry as a light and refreshing meal.

Feel free to customize the recipe by adding other vegetables or adjusting the level of black pepper to suit your taste. It's a perfect dish for a quick and delicious weeknight dinner.

Sweet and Sour Tofu Stir-Fry

Ingredients:

For the Tofu:

- 1 lb (450g) firm tofu, cubed
- 3 tablespoons soy sauce
- 2 tablespoons cornstarch
- Vegetable oil for frying

For the Stir-Fry Sauce:

- 1/4 cup ketchup
- 3 tablespoons rice vinegar
- 2 tablespoons soy sauce
- 2 tablespoons brown sugar
- 1 tablespoon cornstarch
- 1/2 cup pineapple juice (from canned pineapple chunks)

For the Stir-Fry:

- 2 tablespoons vegetable oil
- 1 red bell pepper, sliced
- 1 green bell pepper, sliced
- 1 onion, sliced
- 1 cup pineapple chunks (fresh or canned)
- 1 carrot, julienned
- 3 cloves garlic, minced
- Cooked white or brown rice (for serving)
- Sesame seeds and chopped green onions (for garnish)

Instructions:

Prepare Tofu:
- In a bowl, toss the tofu cubes with soy sauce and cornstarch until well-coated. Heat vegetable oil in a pan over medium-high heat and fry the tofu until golden and crispy. Remove tofu from the pan and set aside on a paper towel.

Prepare Stir-Fry Sauce:

- In a small bowl, whisk together ketchup, rice vinegar, soy sauce, brown sugar, cornstarch, and pineapple juice to make the sweet and sour sauce. Set aside.

Stir-Fry Vegetables:
- In the same pan, add a bit more oil if needed. Sauté sliced red and green bell peppers, onion, julienned carrot, and minced garlic for 3-4 minutes until the vegetables are tender-crisp.

Add Pineapple:
- Add pineapple chunks to the pan and stir well with the vegetables.

Combine Tofu and Vegetables:
- Return the crispy tofu to the pan with the stir-fried vegetables and pineapple.

Pour Stir-Fry Sauce:
- Pour the prepared sweet and sour sauce over the tofu and vegetables. Stir everything well to coat.

Finish Cooking:
- Continue to stir-fry for an additional 2-3 minutes until everything is well-coated and heated through.

Serve:
- Serve the Sweet and Sour Tofu Stir-Fry over cooked white or brown rice.

Garnish:
- Garnish with sesame seeds and chopped green onions on top.

Enjoy:
- Enjoy this sweet, tangy, and crispy Sweet and Sour Tofu Stir-Fry as a delicious and satisfying vegetarian meal.

Feel free to customize the recipe by adding other vegetables or adjusting the sweetness and tanginess of the sauce to your liking. It's a flavorful and colorful dish that's perfect for a meatless dinner option.

Thai Basil Pork Stir-Fry

Ingredients:

For the Sauce:

- 3 tablespoons soy sauce
- 1 tablespoon oyster sauce
- 1 tablespoon fish sauce
- 1 tablespoon sweet soy sauce
- 1 teaspoon sugar

For the Stir-Fry:

- 2 tablespoons vegetable oil
- 4 cloves garlic, minced
- 1-2 red chilies, finely chopped (adjust to taste)
- 1 lb (450g) ground pork
- 1 cup fresh Thai basil leaves
- 1 red bell pepper, thinly sliced
- 1 green bell pepper, thinly sliced
- 2 tablespoons water
- Cooked jasmine rice (for serving)
- Fried egg (optional, for serving)

Instructions:

Prepare Sauce:
- In a bowl, mix together soy sauce, oyster sauce, fish sauce, sweet soy sauce, and sugar. Set aside.

Stir-Fry Pork:
- Heat vegetable oil in a wok or large skillet over medium-high heat. Add minced garlic and chopped red chilies, sauté for about 30 seconds until fragrant. Add ground pork and cook until browned, breaking it apart with a spatula.

Add Bell Peppers:
- Add thinly sliced red and green bell peppers to the wok. Stir-fry for 2-3 minutes until the peppers are slightly tender.

Pour in Sauce:

- Pour the prepared sauce over the pork and bell peppers. Stir well to coat everything in the sauce.

Add Thai Basil:
- Add fresh Thai basil leaves to the wok. Stir-fry for an additional 1-2 minutes until the basil is wilted.

Add Water:
- If the mixture seems too dry, add 2 tablespoons of water to create a bit of sauce. Stir to combine.

Serve:
- Serve the Thai Basil Pork Stir-Fry over cooked jasmine rice.

Optional:
- Top with a fried egg for an extra layer of richness and flavor.

Enjoy:
- Enjoy this aromatic and spicy Thai Basil Pork Stir-Fry as a delicious and satisfying meal.

Feel free to adjust the level of spiciness by adding more or fewer chilies according to your preference. This dish is a classic Thai favorite that's quick and easy to make at home.

Mediterranean Chicken Stir-Fry

Ingredients:

For the Chicken Marinade:

- 1 lb (450g) boneless, skinless chicken breasts, cut into bite-sized strips
- 2 tablespoons olive oil
- 2 tablespoons lemon juice
- 1 teaspoon dried oregano
- 1 teaspoon dried thyme
- Salt and pepper to taste

For the Stir-Fry:

- 2 tablespoons olive oil
- 3 cloves garlic, minced
- 1 red bell pepper, sliced
- 1 yellow bell pepper, sliced
- 1 cup cherry tomatoes, halved
- 1 cup baby spinach leaves
- 1/2 cup Kalamata olives, pitted and sliced
- 1/4 cup crumbled feta cheese
- Lemon wedges (for serving)
- Cooked quinoa or couscous (for serving)

Instructions:

Marinate Chicken:
- In a bowl, combine chicken strips with olive oil, lemon juice, dried oregano, dried thyme, salt, and pepper. Let it marinate for about 15-20 minutes.

Stir-Fry Chicken:
- Heat 2 tablespoons of olive oil in a large skillet or wok over medium-high heat. Add minced garlic and marinated chicken strips. Stir-fry for 5-7 minutes until the chicken is cooked through and browned.

Add Vegetables:
- Add sliced red and yellow bell peppers to the skillet. Stir-fry for an additional 3-4 minutes until the peppers are slightly tender.

Add Tomatoes and Spinach:

- Add halved cherry tomatoes and baby spinach leaves to the skillet. Stir-fry for 2-3 minutes until the spinach wilts and the tomatoes are heated through.

Finish Stir-Fry:
- Stir in sliced Kalamata olives and crumbled feta cheese. Cook for an additional 1-2 minutes until the cheese starts to melt.

Serve:
- Serve the Mediterranean Chicken Stir-Fry over cooked quinoa or couscous.

Garnish:
- Garnish with lemon wedges on the side for squeezing over the dish.

Enjoy:
- Enjoy this vibrant and flavorful Mediterranean Chicken Stir-Fry as a healthy and satisfying meal.

Feel free to customize the recipe by adding other Mediterranean ingredients such as artichoke hearts, sun-dried tomatoes, or capers. It's a versatile dish that captures the essence of Mediterranean cuisine.

Ginger Scallion Beef Stir-Fry

Ingredients:

For the Beef Marinade:

- 1 lb (450g) flank steak, thinly sliced
- 2 tablespoons soy sauce
- 1 tablespoon rice wine or dry sherry
- 1 tablespoon cornstarch

For the Stir-Fry Sauce:

- 3 tablespoons soy sauce
- 1 tablespoon oyster sauce
- 1 tablespoon hoisin sauce
- 1 tablespoon sesame oil
- 1 teaspoon sugar

For the Stir-Fry:

- 2 tablespoons vegetable oil
- 3 tablespoons ginger, julienned
- 4 green onions, sliced (white and green parts separated)
- 1 red bell pepper, thinly sliced
- 1 cup broccoli florets
- Cooked white rice (for serving)
- Sesame seeds (for garnish)

Instructions:

Marinate Beef:
- In a bowl, combine sliced flank steak with soy sauce, rice wine or sherry, and cornstarch. Let it marinate for about 15-20 minutes.

Prepare Stir-Fry Sauce:
- In another bowl, whisk together soy sauce, oyster sauce, hoisin sauce, sesame oil, and sugar to make the sauce. Set aside.

Stir-Fry Beef:
- Heat vegetable oil in a wok or large skillet over medium-high heat. Add julienned ginger and the white parts of the sliced green onions. Sauté for about 30 seconds until fragrant. Add the marinated beef slices and stir-fry

for 2-3 minutes until they are browned and cooked through. Remove beef from the pan and set aside.

Stir-Fry Vegetables:
- In the same pan, add a bit more oil if needed. Add sliced red bell pepper and broccoli florets. Stir-fry for 3-4 minutes until the vegetables are tender-crisp.

Combine Beef and Vegetables:
- Return the cooked beef to the pan with the stir-fried vegetables.

Add Sauce:
- Pour the prepared stir-fry sauce over the beef and vegetables. Stir everything well to coat in the sauce.

Finish Cooking:
- Continue to stir-fry for an additional 2-3 minutes until everything is heated through and well-coated.

Serve:
- Serve the Ginger Scallion Beef Stir-Fry over cooked white rice.

Garnish:
- Garnish with the green parts of the sliced green onions and sprinkle sesame seeds on top.

Enjoy:
- Enjoy this aromatic and savory Ginger Scallion Beef Stir-Fry as a delicious and quick meal.

Feel free to customize the recipe by adding other vegetables or adjusting the level of ginger and scallions to suit your taste. It's a classic Asian stir-fry that's both flavorful and satisfying.

Hoisin Glazed Vegetable Stir-Fry

Ingredients:

For the Stir-Fry Sauce:

- 3 tablespoons hoisin sauce
- 2 tablespoons soy sauce
- 1 tablespoon rice vinegar
- 1 tablespoon sesame oil
- 1 tablespoon honey or maple syrup
- 1 teaspoon cornstarch

For the Stir-Fry:

- 2 tablespoons vegetable oil
- 3 cloves garlic, minced
- 1 tablespoon fresh ginger, grated
- 1 red bell pepper, sliced
- 1 yellow bell pepper, sliced
- 1 carrot, julienned
- 1 zucchini, sliced
- 1 cup broccoli florets
- 1 cup snap peas, ends trimmed
- 1 cup baby corn, halved
- Sesame seeds (for garnish)
- Cooked rice or noodles (for serving)

Instructions:

Prepare Stir-Fry Sauce:
- In a bowl, whisk together hoisin sauce, soy sauce, rice vinegar, sesame oil, honey or maple syrup, and cornstarch. Set aside.

Stir-Fry Vegetables:
- Heat vegetable oil in a wok or large skillet over medium-high heat. Add minced garlic and grated ginger, sauté for about 30 seconds until fragrant.

Add Vegetables:
- Add sliced red and yellow bell peppers, julienned carrot, sliced zucchini, broccoli florets, snap peas, and baby corn to the wok. Stir-fry for 4-5 minutes until the vegetables are tender-crisp.

Add Sauce:
- Pour the prepared stir-fry sauce over the vegetables. Stir everything well to coat the vegetables evenly.

Finish Stir-Fry:
- Continue to stir-fry for an additional 2-3 minutes until the sauce thickens and coats the vegetables.

Serve:
- Serve the Hoisin Glazed Vegetable Stir-Fry over cooked rice or noodles.

Garnish:
- Garnish with sesame seeds on top for added texture and flavor.

Enjoy:
- Enjoy this flavorful and saucy Hoisin Glazed Vegetable Stir-Fry as a delicious and satisfying meal.

Feel free to customize the recipe by adding tofu, chicken, or shrimp for added protein. The hoisin sauce brings a rich and savory flavor to the dish, making it a tasty and quick option for a weeknight dinner.

Cajun Shrimp and Sausage Stir-Fry

Ingredients:

For the Cajun Seasoning:

- 1 tablespoon paprika
- 1 tablespoon onion powder
- 1 tablespoon garlic powder
- 1 teaspoon thyme
- 1 teaspoon oregano
- 1 teaspoon cayenne pepper (adjust to taste)
- Salt and black pepper to taste

For the Stir-Fry:

- 1 lb (450g) large shrimp, peeled and deveined
- 1/2 lb (225g) smoked sausage, sliced
- 2 tablespoons Cajun seasoning (divided)
- 2 tablespoons vegetable oil
- 1 red bell pepper, sliced
- 1 green bell pepper, sliced
- 1 onion, thinly sliced
- 3 cloves garlic, minced
- Cooked rice or pasta (for serving)
- Chopped green onions (for garnish)

Instructions:

Prepare Cajun Seasoning:
- In a bowl, mix together paprika, onion powder, garlic powder, thyme, oregano, cayenne pepper, salt, and black pepper. Set aside.

Season Shrimp and Sausage:
- In a separate bowl, toss the shrimp and sliced smoked sausage with 1 tablespoon of the Cajun seasoning, ensuring they are well coated.

Cook Shrimp and Sausage:
- Heat vegetable oil in a large skillet or wok over medium-high heat. Add the seasoned shrimp and sausage to the pan and cook for 3-4 minutes until the shrimp is pink and opaque, and the sausage is browned. Remove from the pan and set aside.

Stir-Fry Vegetables:
- In the same pan, add a bit more oil if needed. Add sliced red and green bell peppers, thinly sliced onion, and minced garlic. Stir-fry for 3-4 minutes until the vegetables are tender-crisp.

Combine Shrimp, Sausage, and Vegetables:
- Return the cooked shrimp and sausage to the pan with the stir-fried vegetables.

Add Cajun Seasoning:
- Sprinkle the remaining 1 tablespoon of Cajun seasoning over the ingredients. Stir everything well to combine.

Finish Cooking:
- Continue to stir-fry for an additional 2-3 minutes until everything is heated through and well-coated in the Cajun seasoning.

Serve:
- Serve the Cajun Shrimp and Sausage Stir-Fry over cooked rice or pasta.

Garnish:
- Garnish with chopped green onions on top.

Enjoy:
- Enjoy this spicy and flavorful Cajun Shrimp and Sausage Stir-Fry as a delicious and satisfying meal.

Feel free to adjust the level of spiciness by adding more or less cayenne pepper to suit your taste. It's a quick and hearty dish that brings a taste of Cajun cuisine to your table.

Black Bean Garlic Chicken Stir-Fry

Ingredients:

For the Marinade:

- 1 lb (450g) boneless, skinless chicken thighs, thinly sliced
- 2 tablespoons soy sauce
- 1 tablespoon oyster sauce
- 1 tablespoon rice wine or dry sherry
- 1 tablespoon cornstarch

For the Stir-Fry Sauce:

- 2 tablespoons black bean garlic sauce
- 1 tablespoon soy sauce
- 1 tablespoon oyster sauce
- 1 teaspoon sugar

For the Stir-Fry:

- 2 tablespoons vegetable oil
- 4 cloves garlic, minced
- 1 tablespoon fresh ginger, grated
- 1 red bell pepper, sliced
- 1 yellow bell pepper, sliced
- 1 cup broccoli florets
- 1 carrot, julienned
- Cooked white rice (for serving)
- Green onions, sliced (for garnish)

Instructions:

Marinate Chicken:
- In a bowl, combine sliced chicken with soy sauce, oyster sauce, rice wine or sherry, and cornstarch. Let it marinate for about 15-20 minutes.

Prepare Stir-Fry Sauce:
- In another bowl, mix together black bean garlic sauce, soy sauce, oyster sauce, and sugar. Set aside.

Stir-Fry Chicken:

- Heat vegetable oil in a wok or large skillet over medium-high heat. Add minced garlic and grated ginger, sauté for about 30 seconds until fragrant. Add the marinated chicken slices and stir-fry for 3-4 minutes until they are browned and cooked through. Remove chicken from the pan and set aside.

Stir-Fry Vegetables:
- In the same pan, add a bit more oil if needed. Add sliced red and yellow bell peppers, broccoli florets, and julienned carrot. Stir-fry for 3-4 minutes until the vegetables are tender-crisp.

Combine Chicken and Vegetables:
- Return the cooked chicken to the pan with the stir-fried vegetables.

Add Stir-Fry Sauce:
- Pour the prepared stir-fry sauce over the chicken and vegetables. Stir everything well to coat in the sauce.

Finish Stir-Fry:
- Continue to stir-fry for an additional 2-3 minutes until everything is heated through and well-coated.

Serve:
- Serve the Black Bean Garlic Chicken Stir-Fry over cooked white rice.

Garnish:
- Garnish with sliced green onions on top.

Enjoy:
- Enjoy this savory and aromatic Black Bean Garlic Chicken Stir-Fry as a delicious and quick meal.

Feel free to customize the recipe by adding other vegetables or adjusting the level of garlic and black bean sauce to suit your taste. It's a classic stir-fry that brings bold flavors to the table.

Spicy Teriyaki Tofu Stir-Fry

Ingredients:

For the Teriyaki Sauce:

- 1/4 cup soy sauce
- 2 tablespoons mirin (sweet rice wine)
- 2 tablespoons sake or dry sherry
- 2 tablespoons brown sugar
- 1 teaspoon sesame oil
- 1 teaspoon grated ginger
- 1 teaspoon cornstarch

For the Stir-Fry:

- 1 block extra-firm tofu, pressed and cubed
- 2 tablespoons vegetable oil
- 3 cloves garlic, minced
- 1 tablespoon fresh ginger, grated
- 1 red bell pepper, sliced
- 1 yellow bell pepper, sliced
- 1 cup broccoli florets
- 1 carrot, julienned
- 1-2 red chili peppers, sliced (adjust to taste)
- Cooked brown rice or noodles (for serving)
- Sesame seeds and chopped green onions (for garnish)

Instructions:

Prepare Teriyaki Sauce:
- In a bowl, whisk together soy sauce, mirin, sake or sherry, brown sugar, sesame oil, grated ginger, and cornstarch. Set aside.

Press and Cube Tofu:
- Press the tofu to remove excess water and cut it into cubes.

Stir-Fry Tofu:
- Heat vegetable oil in a wok or large skillet over medium-high heat. Add cubed tofu and cook until golden brown on all sides. Remove tofu from the pan and set aside.

Sauté Garlic and Ginger:

- In the same pan, add a bit more oil if needed. Add minced garlic and grated ginger, sauté for about 30 seconds until fragrant.

Add Vegetables:
- Add sliced red and yellow bell peppers, broccoli florets, julienned carrot, and sliced red chili peppers to the pan. Stir-fry for 3-4 minutes until the vegetables are tender-crisp.

Combine Tofu and Vegetables:
- Return the cooked tofu to the pan with the stir-fried vegetables.

Pour Teriyaki Sauce:
- Pour the prepared teriyaki sauce over the tofu and vegetables. Stir everything well to coat in the sauce.

Finish Stir-Fry:
- Continue to stir-fry for an additional 2-3 minutes until everything is heated through and well-coated.

Serve:
- Serve the Spicy Teriyaki Tofu Stir-Fry over cooked brown rice or noodles.

Garnish:
- Garnish with sesame seeds and chopped green onions on top.

Enjoy:
- Enjoy this Spicy Teriyaki Tofu Stir-Fry as a delicious and satisfying vegetarian meal.

Feel free to adjust the level of spiciness by adding more or fewer chili peppers according to your preference. This flavorful stir-fry is a great way to enjoy a tasty and healthy dish.

Lemon Garlic Vegetable Stir-Fry

Ingredients:

For the Stir-Fry Sauce:

- 3 tablespoons soy sauce
- 2 tablespoons fresh lemon juice
- 1 tablespoon honey or maple syrup
- 1 teaspoon cornstarch

For the Stir-Fry:

- 2 tablespoons vegetable oil
- 3 cloves garlic, minced
- 1 tablespoon fresh ginger, grated
- 1 red bell pepper, sliced
- 1 yellow bell pepper, sliced
- 1 cup broccoli florets
- 1 carrot, julienned
- 1 zucchini, sliced
- 1 cup snap peas, ends trimmed
- Zest of one lemon
- Cooked quinoa or rice (for serving)
- Chopped cilantro or parsley (for garnish)

Instructions:

Prepare Stir-Fry Sauce:
- In a bowl, whisk together soy sauce, fresh lemon juice, honey or maple syrup, and cornstarch. Set aside.

Stir-Fry Vegetables:
- Heat vegetable oil in a wok or large skillet over medium-high heat. Add minced garlic and grated ginger, sauté for about 30 seconds until fragrant.

Add Vegetables:
- Add sliced red and yellow bell peppers, broccoli florets, julienned carrot, sliced zucchini, and snap peas to the wok. Stir-fry for 4-5 minutes until the vegetables are tender-crisp.

Pour Stir-Fry Sauce:
- Pour the prepared stir-fry sauce over the vegetables. Stir everything well to coat the vegetables evenly.

Add Lemon Zest:
- Add the zest of one lemon to the pan. Stir to combine.

Finish Stir-Fry:
- Continue to stir-fry for an additional 2-3 minutes until the sauce thickens and coats the vegetables.

Serve:
- Serve the Lemon Garlic Vegetable Stir-Fry over cooked quinoa or rice.

Garnish:
- Garnish with chopped cilantro or parsley on top.

Enjoy:
- Enjoy this light and citrusy Lemon Garlic Vegetable Stir-Fry as a flavorful and healthy meal.

Feel free to customize the recipe by adding other vegetables or proteins of your choice.

The lemon and garlic combination adds a refreshing twist to the classic vegetable stir-fry.

Sesame Orange Tofu Stir-Fry

Ingredients:

For the Stir-Fry Sauce:

- 1/4 cup soy sauce
- 3 tablespoons orange juice
- 2 tablespoons rice vinegar
- 2 tablespoons sesame oil
- 2 tablespoons maple syrup or honey
- 1 tablespoon cornstarch

For the Stir-Fry:

- 1 block extra-firm tofu, pressed and cubed
- 2 tablespoons vegetable oil
- 3 cloves garlic, minced
- 1 tablespoon fresh ginger, grated
- 1 red bell pepper, sliced
- 1 yellow bell pepper, sliced
- 1 cup broccoli florets
- 1 carrot, julienned
- Cooked brown rice or noodles (for serving)
- Sesame seeds and sliced green onions (for garnish)

Instructions:

Prepare Stir-Fry Sauce:
- In a bowl, whisk together soy sauce, orange juice, rice vinegar, sesame oil, maple syrup or honey, and cornstarch. Set aside.

Press and Cube Tofu:
- Press the tofu to remove excess water and cut it into cubes.

Stir-Fry Tofu:
- Heat vegetable oil in a wok or large skillet over medium-high heat. Add cubed tofu and cook until golden brown on all sides. Remove tofu from the pan and set aside.

Sauté Garlic and Ginger:
- In the same pan, add a bit more oil if needed. Add minced garlic and grated ginger, sauté for about 30 seconds until fragrant.

Add Vegetables:

- Add sliced red and yellow bell peppers, broccoli florets, julienned carrot to the pan. Stir-fry for 3-4 minutes until the vegetables are tender-crisp.

Combine Tofu and Vegetables:
- Return the cooked tofu to the pan with the stir-fried vegetables.

Pour Stir-Fry Sauce:
- Pour the prepared stir-fry sauce over the tofu and vegetables. Stir everything well to coat in the sauce.

Finish Stir-Fry:
- Continue to stir-fry for an additional 2-3 minutes until everything is heated through and well-coated.

Serve:
- Serve the Sesame Orange Tofu Stir-Fry over cooked brown rice or noodles.

Garnish:
- Garnish with sesame seeds and sliced green onions on top.

Enjoy:
- Enjoy this Sesame Orange Tofu Stir-Fry as a flavorful and satisfying vegetarian meal.

Feel free to adjust the sweetness or tartness of the sauce to suit your taste. This stir-fry is a perfect balance of savory, citrusy, and nutty flavors.

Coconut Curry Chicken Stir-Fry

Ingredients:

For the Curry Sauce:

- 1 cup coconut milk
- 2 tablespoons red curry paste
- 1 tablespoon soy sauce
- 1 tablespoon fish sauce (optional for non-vegetarian version)
- 1 tablespoon brown sugar
- 1 teaspoon ground turmeric
- 1 teaspoon ground coriander
- 1 teaspoon chili flakes (adjust to taste)

For the Stir-Fry:

- 1 lb (450g) boneless, skinless chicken breasts, thinly sliced
- 2 tablespoons vegetable oil
- 1 onion, thinly sliced
- 1 red bell pepper, sliced
- 1 yellow bell pepper, sliced
- 1 cup snap peas, ends trimmed
- 3 cloves garlic, minced
- 1 tablespoon fresh ginger, grated
- Cooked jasmine rice or noodles (for serving)
- Fresh cilantro leaves (for garnish)
- Lime wedges (for serving)

Instructions:

Prepare Curry Sauce:
- In a bowl, whisk together coconut milk, red curry paste, soy sauce, fish sauce (if using), brown sugar, ground turmeric, ground coriander, and chili flakes. Set aside.

Stir-Fry Chicken:
- Heat vegetable oil in a wok or large skillet over medium-high heat. Add sliced chicken and cook until browned and cooked through. Remove chicken from the pan and set aside.

Sauté Onion, Bell Peppers, and Snap Peas:

- In the same pan, add a bit more oil if needed. Add sliced onion, red bell pepper, yellow bell pepper, and snap peas. Stir-fry for 3-4 minutes until the vegetables are tender-crisp.

Add Garlic and Ginger:
- Add minced garlic and grated ginger to the pan. Sauté for about 30 seconds until fragrant.

Combine Chicken and Vegetables:
- Return the cooked chicken to the pan with the sautéed vegetables.

Pour Curry Sauce:
- Pour the prepared curry sauce over the chicken and vegetables. Stir everything well to coat in the sauce.

Finish Stir-Fry:
- Continue to stir-fry for an additional 2-3 minutes until everything is heated through and well-coated.

Serve:
- Serve the Coconut Curry Chicken Stir-Fry over cooked jasmine rice or noodles.

Garnish:
- Garnish with fresh cilantro leaves on top.

Squeeze Lime:
- Squeeze lime wedges over the dish before serving for an extra burst of freshness.

Enjoy:
- Enjoy this Coconut Curry Chicken Stir-Fry as a delicious and aromatic meal.

Feel free to adjust the level of spiciness and sweetness according to your taste preferences. This stir-fry brings a delightful combination of creamy coconut and savory curry flavors.

Peanut Noodle Stir-Fry

Ingredients:

For the Peanut Sauce:

- 1/2 cup peanut butter
- 3 tablespoons soy sauce
- 2 tablespoons rice vinegar
- 1 tablespoon sesame oil
- 1 tablespoon honey or maple syrup
- 1 clove garlic, minced
- 1 teaspoon fresh ginger, grated
- 1 teaspoon chili garlic sauce (adjust to taste)
- 1/4 cup warm water (as needed to thin the sauce)

For the Stir-Fry:

- 8 oz (225g) rice noodles or soba noodles
- 2 tablespoons vegetable oil
- 1 red bell pepper, sliced
- 1 yellow bell pepper, sliced
- 1 carrot, julienned
- 1 cup snap peas, ends trimmed
- 3 green onions, sliced
- Sesame seeds and chopped peanuts (for garnish)
- Lime wedges (for serving)

Instructions:

Prepare Peanut Sauce:
- In a bowl, whisk together peanut butter, soy sauce, rice vinegar, sesame oil, honey or maple syrup, minced garlic, grated ginger, and chili garlic sauce. If the sauce is too thick, add warm water gradually until you achieve the desired consistency. Set aside.

Cook Noodles:
- Cook rice noodles or soba noodles according to package instructions. Drain and set aside.

Stir-Fry Vegetables:

- Heat vegetable oil in a wok or large skillet over medium-high heat. Add sliced red and yellow bell peppers, julienned carrot, snap peas, and sliced green onions. Stir-fry for 3-4 minutes until the vegetables are tender-crisp.

Combine Noodles and Vegetables:
- Add the cooked noodles to the wok with the stir-fried vegetables. Toss everything together to combine.

Add Peanut Sauce:
- Pour the prepared peanut sauce over the noodles and vegetables. Toss everything well to coat in the sauce.

Finish Stir-Fry:
- Continue to stir-fry for an additional 2-3 minutes until everything is heated through and well-coated.

Serve:
- Serve the Peanut Noodle Stir-Fry in bowls.

Garnish:
- Garnish with sesame seeds and chopped peanuts on top.

Squeeze Lime:
- Squeeze lime wedges over the dish before serving for an extra burst of freshness.

Enjoy:
- Enjoy this Peanut Noodle Stir-Fry as a delicious and flavorful meal.

Feel free to customize the recipe by adding protein such as tofu, chicken, or shrimp. The creamy peanut sauce adds richness to the noodles, making it a satisfying and tasty dish.

Hoisin Pork and Broccoli Stir-Fry

Ingredients:

For the Marinade:

- 1 lb (450g) pork tenderloin or pork loin, thinly sliced
- 2 tablespoons soy sauce
- 1 tablespoon rice vinegar
- 1 tablespoon hoisin sauce
- 1 tablespoon cornstarch

For the Stir-Fry Sauce:

- 3 tablespoons hoisin sauce
- 2 tablespoons soy sauce
- 1 tablespoon oyster sauce
- 1 tablespoon sesame oil
- 1 tablespoon brown sugar

For the Stir-Fry:

- 2 tablespoons vegetable oil
- 3 cloves garlic, minced
- 1 tablespoon fresh ginger, grated
- 1 broccoli crown, cut into florets
- Cooked white or brown rice (for serving)
- Sesame seeds and sliced green onions (for garnish)

Instructions:

Marinate Pork:
- In a bowl, combine sliced pork with soy sauce, rice vinegar, hoisin sauce, and cornstarch. Let it marinate for about 15-20 minutes.

Prepare Stir-Fry Sauce:
- In another bowl, whisk together hoisin sauce, soy sauce, oyster sauce, sesame oil, and brown sugar. Set aside.

Stir-Fry Pork:
- Heat vegetable oil in a wok or large skillet over medium-high heat. Add marinated pork slices and stir-fry until browned and cooked through. Remove pork from the pan and set aside.

Sauté Garlic and Ginger:
- In the same pan, add a bit more oil if needed. Add minced garlic and grated ginger, sauté for about 30 seconds until fragrant.

Stir-Fry Broccoli:
- Add broccoli florets to the pan. Stir-fry for 3-4 minutes until the broccoli is tender-crisp.

Combine Pork and Broccoli:
- Return the cooked pork to the pan with the stir-fried broccoli.

Pour Stir-Fry Sauce:
- Pour the prepared stir-fry sauce over the pork and broccoli. Stir everything well to coat in the sauce.

Finish Stir-Fry:
- Continue to stir-fry for an additional 2-3 minutes until everything is heated through and well-coated.

Serve:
- Serve the Hoisin Pork and Broccoli Stir-Fry over cooked white or brown rice.

Garnish:
- Garnish with sesame seeds and sliced green onions on top.

Enjoy:
- Enjoy this Hoisin Pork and Broccoli Stir-Fry as a delicious and quick meal.

Feel free to adjust the sweetness or saltiness of the sauce according to your taste preferences. This stir-fry is a delightful combination of tender pork, crisp broccoli, and flavorful hoisin sauce.

Five-Spice Shrimp Stir-Fry

Ingredients:

For the Marinade:

- 1 lb (450g) large shrimp, peeled and deveined
- 2 tablespoons soy sauce
- 1 tablespoon rice wine or dry sherry
- 1 tablespoon cornstarch
- 1 teaspoon Chinese five-spice powder

For the Stir-Fry Sauce:

- 3 tablespoons oyster sauce
- 2 tablespoons soy sauce
- 1 tablespoon hoisin sauce
- 1 tablespoon rice vinegar
- 1 tablespoon sesame oil
- 1 tablespoon brown sugar

For the Stir-Fry:

- 2 tablespoons vegetable oil
- 3 cloves garlic, minced
- 1 tablespoon fresh ginger, grated
- 1 red bell pepper, sliced
- 1 yellow bell pepper, sliced
- 1 cup snap peas, ends trimmed
- Cooked jasmine rice or noodles (for serving)
- Sesame seeds and sliced green onions (for garnish)

Instructions:

Marinate Shrimp:
- In a bowl, combine shrimp with soy sauce, rice wine or sherry, cornstarch, and Chinese five-spice powder. Let it marinate for about 15-20 minutes.

Prepare Stir-Fry Sauce:
- In another bowl, whisk together oyster sauce, soy sauce, hoisin sauce, rice vinegar, sesame oil, and brown sugar. Set aside.

Stir-Fry Shrimp:

- Heat vegetable oil in a wok or large skillet over medium-high heat. Add marinated shrimp and stir-fry until they turn pink and opaque. Remove shrimp from the pan and set aside.

Sauté Garlic and Ginger:
- In the same pan, add a bit more oil if needed. Add minced garlic and grated ginger, sauté for about 30 seconds until fragrant.

Stir-Fry Vegetables:
- Add sliced red and yellow bell peppers, and snap peas to the pan. Stir-fry for 3-4 minutes until the vegetables are tender-crisp.

Combine Shrimp and Vegetables:
- Return the cooked shrimp to the pan with the stir-fried vegetables.

Pour Stir-Fry Sauce:
- Pour the prepared stir-fry sauce over the shrimp and vegetables. Stir everything well to coat in the sauce.

Finish Stir-Fry:
- Continue to stir-fry for an additional 2-3 minutes until everything is heated through and well-coated.

Serve:
- Serve the Five-Spice Shrimp Stir-Fry over cooked jasmine rice or noodles.

Garnish:
- Garnish with sesame seeds and sliced green onions on top.

Enjoy:
- Enjoy this Five-Spice Shrimp Stir-Fry as a flavorful and aromatic meal.

Feel free to customize the recipe by adding more vegetables or adjusting the level of Chinese five-spice powder to suit your taste. This stir-fry offers a delightful blend of spices with succulent shrimp and crisp vegetables.

Soy Ginger Mushroom Stir-Fry

Ingredients:

For the Stir-Fry Sauce:

- 3 tablespoons soy sauce
- 2 tablespoons rice vinegar
- 1 tablespoon sesame oil
- 1 tablespoon hoisin sauce
- 1 tablespoon brown sugar
- 1 tablespoon cornstarch

For the Stir-Fry:

- 2 tablespoons vegetable oil
- 1 lb (450g) mixed mushrooms (such as shiitake, cremini, or oyster), sliced
- 3 cloves garlic, minced
- 1 tablespoon fresh ginger, grated
- 1 red bell pepper, sliced
- 1 yellow bell pepper, sliced
- 1 cup snap peas, ends trimmed
- Cooked brown rice or noodles (for serving)
- Sesame seeds and sliced green onions (for garnish)

Instructions:

Prepare Stir-Fry Sauce:
- In a bowl, whisk together soy sauce, rice vinegar, sesame oil, hoisin sauce, brown sugar, and cornstarch. Set aside.

Stir-Fry Mushrooms:
- Heat vegetable oil in a wok or large skillet over medium-high heat. Add sliced mushrooms and stir-fry until they release their moisture and become golden brown.

Sauté Garlic and Ginger:
- Push the mushrooms to the side of the pan and add minced garlic and grated ginger. Sauté for about 30 seconds until fragrant.

Stir-Fry Vegetables:
- Add sliced red and yellow bell peppers, and snap peas to the pan with the mushrooms. Stir-fry for 3-4 minutes until the vegetables are tender-crisp.

Combine Stir-Fry Sauce:

- Pour the prepared stir-fry sauce over the mushrooms and vegetables. Stir everything well to coat in the sauce.

Finish Stir-Fry:
- Continue to stir-fry for an additional 2-3 minutes until everything is heated through and well-coated.

Serve:
- Serve the Soy Ginger Mushroom Stir-Fry over cooked brown rice or noodles.

Garnish:
- Garnish with sesame seeds and sliced green onions on top.

Enjoy:
- Enjoy this Soy Ginger Mushroom Stir-Fry as a flavorful and hearty vegetarian meal.

Feel free to customize the recipe by adding tofu, tempeh, or your favorite protein. The combination of mushrooms, soy, and ginger creates a deliciously savory stir-fry that's perfect for a quick and nutritious meal.

Teriyaki Beef and Mushroom Stir-Fry

Ingredients:

For the Teriyaki Sauce:

- 1/2 cup soy sauce
- 3 tablespoons mirin
- 2 tablespoons sake (or dry sherry)
- 2 tablespoons brown sugar
- 1 tablespoon honey
- 1 teaspoon sesame oil
- 1 teaspoon cornstarch dissolved in 2 tablespoons water

For the Stir-Fry:

- 1 lb (450g) flank steak, thinly sliced
- 2 tablespoons vegetable oil
- 1 lb (450g) mixed mushrooms (such as shiitake, cremini, or oyster), sliced
- 3 cloves garlic, minced
- 1 tablespoon fresh ginger, grated
- 1 red bell pepper, sliced
- 1 cup snow peas, ends trimmed
- Cooked jasmine rice or noodles (for serving)
- Sesame seeds and sliced green onions (for garnish)

Instructions:

Prepare Teriyaki Sauce:
- In a bowl, whisk together soy sauce, mirin, sake, brown sugar, honey, sesame oil, and the cornstarch-water mixture. Set aside.

Marinate Beef:
- Place thinly sliced flank steak in a bowl and pour a couple of tablespoons of the teriyaki sauce over it. Allow the beef to marinate for about 15-20 minutes.

Stir-Fry Beef:
- Heat vegetable oil in a wok or large skillet over medium-high heat. Add the marinated beef and stir-fry until it is browned and cooked to your liking. Remove the beef from the pan and set aside.

Sauté Garlic and Ginger:

- In the same pan, add a bit more oil if needed. Add minced garlic and grated ginger, sauté for about 30 seconds until fragrant.

Stir-Fry Mushrooms and Vegetables:
- Add sliced mushrooms, red bell pepper, and snow peas to the pan. Stir-fry for 3-4 minutes until the vegetables are tender-crisp.

Combine Beef and Vegetables:
- Return the cooked beef to the pan with the stir-fried vegetables.

Pour Teriyaki Sauce:
- Pour the remaining teriyaki sauce over the beef and vegetables. Stir everything well to coat in the sauce.

Finish Stir-Fry:
- Continue to stir-fry for an additional 2-3 minutes until everything is heated through and well-coated.

Serve:
- Serve the Teriyaki Beef and Mushroom Stir-Fry over cooked jasmine rice or noodles.

Garnish:
- Garnish with sesame seeds and sliced green onions on top.

Enjoy:
- Enjoy this Teriyaki Beef and Mushroom Stir-Fry as a flavorful and satisfying meal.

Feel free to customize the recipe by adding your favorite vegetables or adjusting the sweetness and saltiness of the teriyaki sauce to suit your taste. This stir-fry is a perfect balance of savory and sweet flavors.

Lemon Honey Chicken Stir-Fry

Ingredients:

For the Marinade:

- 1 lb (450g) boneless, skinless chicken breasts, thinly sliced
- 2 tablespoons soy sauce
- 1 tablespoon rice vinegar
- 1 tablespoon cornstarch

For the Stir-Fry Sauce:

- 1/4 cup chicken broth
- 2 tablespoons soy sauce
- 2 tablespoons honey
- 2 tablespoons lemon juice
- 1 tablespoon cornstarch

For the Stir-Fry:

- 2 tablespoons vegetable oil
- 3 cloves garlic, minced
- 1 tablespoon fresh ginger, grated
- 1 red bell pepper, sliced
- 1 yellow bell pepper, sliced
- 1 cup broccoli florets
- Zest of 1 lemon
- Cooked jasmine rice or noodles (for serving)
- Sesame seeds and sliced green onions (for garnish)

Instructions:

Marinate Chicken:
- In a bowl, combine sliced chicken with soy sauce, rice vinegar, and cornstarch. Allow the chicken to marinate for about 15-20 minutes.

Prepare Stir-Fry Sauce:
- In another bowl, whisk together chicken broth, soy sauce, honey, lemon juice, and cornstarch. Set aside.

Stir-Fry Chicken:

- Heat vegetable oil in a wok or large skillet over medium-high heat. Add the marinated chicken and stir-fry until it is browned and cooked through. Remove the chicken from the pan and set aside.

Sauté Garlic and Ginger:
- In the same pan, add a bit more oil if needed. Add minced garlic and grated ginger, sauté for about 30 seconds until fragrant.

Stir-Fry Vegetables:
- Add sliced red and yellow bell peppers, broccoli florets, and lemon zest to the pan. Stir-fry for 3-4 minutes until the vegetables are tender-crisp.

Combine Chicken and Vegetables:
- Return the cooked chicken to the pan with the stir-fried vegetables.

Pour Stir-Fry Sauce:
- Pour the prepared stir-fry sauce over the chicken and vegetables. Stir everything well to coat in the sauce.

Finish Stir-Fry:
- Continue to stir-fry for an additional 2-3 minutes until everything is heated through and well-coated.

Serve:
- Serve the Lemon Honey Chicken Stir-Fry over cooked jasmine rice or noodles.

Garnish:
- Garnish with sesame seeds and sliced green onions on top.

Enjoy:
- Enjoy this Lemon Honey Chicken Stir-Fry as a refreshing and flavorful meal.

Feel free to adjust the level of sweetness or tartness by modifying the amount of honey or lemon juice according to your taste preferences. This stir-fry offers a perfect balance of citrusy and sweet flavors.

Korean BBQ Tofu Stir-Fry

Ingredients:

For the Tofu Marinade:

- 1 block extra-firm tofu, pressed and cubed
- 3 tablespoons soy sauce
- 2 tablespoons Korean gochujang (red pepper paste)
- 2 tablespoons rice vinegar
- 1 tablespoon sesame oil
- 1 tablespoon brown sugar
- 1 tablespoon minced garlic
- 1 tablespoon grated ginger

For the Stir-Fry:

- 2 tablespoons vegetable oil
- 1 red bell pepper, sliced
- 1 yellow bell pepper, sliced
- 1 cup broccoli florets
- 1 carrot, julienned
- 1 cup snap peas, ends trimmed
- Cooked jasmine rice (for serving)
- Sesame seeds and sliced green onions (for garnish)

Instructions:

Prepare Tofu Marinade:
- In a bowl, whisk together soy sauce, gochujang, rice vinegar, sesame oil, brown sugar, minced garlic, and grated ginger to create the marinade.

Marinate Tofu:
- Place the cubed tofu in a shallow dish and pour half of the marinade over it. Allow the tofu to marinate for at least 15-20 minutes.

Sauté Tofu:
- Heat vegetable oil in a wok or large skillet over medium-high heat. Add the marinated tofu cubes and sauté until they are golden brown on all sides. Remove tofu from the pan and set aside.

Stir-Fry Vegetables:

- In the same pan, add a bit more oil if needed. Add sliced red and yellow bell peppers, broccoli florets, julienned carrot, and snap peas. Stir-fry for 3-4 minutes until the vegetables are tender-crisp.

Combine Tofu and Vegetables:
- Return the cooked tofu to the pan with the stir-fried vegetables.

Pour Remaining Marinade:
- Pour the remaining tofu marinade over the tofu and vegetables. Stir everything well to coat in the sauce.

Finish Stir-Fry:
- Continue to stir-fry for an additional 2-3 minutes until everything is heated through and well-coated.

Serve:
- Serve the Korean BBQ Tofu Stir-Fry over cooked jasmine rice.

Garnish:
- Garnish with sesame seeds and sliced green onions on top.

Enjoy:
- Enjoy this Korean BBQ Tofu Stir-Fry as a flavorful and satisfying vegetarian meal.

Feel free to adjust the level of spiciness by adding more or less gochujang, according to your taste preferences. This stir-fry captures the bold and delicious flavors of Korean barbecue in a tofu-based dish.

Garlic Ginger Vegetable Stir-Fry

Ingredients:

For the Stir-Fry Sauce:

- 3 tablespoons soy sauce
- 2 tablespoons rice vinegar
- 1 tablespoon sesame oil
- 1 tablespoon hoisin sauce
- 1 tablespoon brown sugar
- 1 tablespoon cornstarch

For the Stir-Fry:

- 2 tablespoons vegetable oil
- 3 cloves garlic, minced
- 1 tablespoon fresh ginger, grated
- 1 broccoli crown, cut into florets
- 1 red bell pepper, sliced
- 1 yellow bell pepper, sliced
- 1 carrot, julienned
- 1 cup snap peas, ends trimmed
- Cooked jasmine rice or noodles (for serving)
- Sesame seeds and sliced green onions (for garnish)

Instructions:

Prepare Stir-Fry Sauce:
- In a bowl, whisk together soy sauce, rice vinegar, sesame oil, hoisin sauce, brown sugar, and cornstarch. Set aside.

Sauté Garlic and Ginger:
- Heat vegetable oil in a wok or large skillet over medium-high heat. Add minced garlic and grated ginger, sauté for about 30 seconds until fragrant.

Stir-Fry Vegetables:
- Add broccoli florets, sliced red and yellow bell peppers, julienned carrot, and snap peas to the pan. Stir-fry for 3-4 minutes until the vegetables are tender-crisp.

Pour Stir-Fry Sauce:
- Pour the prepared stir-fry sauce over the vegetables. Stir everything well to coat in the sauce.

Finish Stir-Fry:
- Continue to stir-fry for an additional 2-3 minutes until everything is heated through and well-coated.

Serve:
- Serve the Garlic Ginger Vegetable Stir-Fry over cooked jasmine rice or noodles.

Garnish:
- Garnish with sesame seeds and sliced green onions on top.

Enjoy:
- Enjoy this Garlic Ginger Vegetable Stir-Fry as a quick, tasty, and wholesome meal.

Feel free to customize the recipe by adding your favorite vegetables or protein sources. The garlic and ginger infusion adds depth of flavor to the colorful assortment of vegetables, making this stir-fry a delightful and healthy option.

Thai Peanut Chicken Stir-Fry

Ingredients:

For the Peanut Sauce:

- 1/3 cup creamy peanut butter
- 3 tablespoons soy sauce
- 2 tablespoons honey
- 2 tablespoons rice vinegar
- 1 tablespoon sesame oil
- 1 tablespoon freshly squeezed lime juice
- 2 cloves garlic, minced
- 1 teaspoon grated ginger
- 1 teaspoon sriracha sauce (optional, for heat)
- 2 tablespoons water (as needed to adjust consistency)

For the Stir-Fry:

- 1 lb (450g) boneless, skinless chicken breasts, thinly sliced
- 2 tablespoons vegetable oil
- 1 red bell pepper, sliced
- 1 yellow bell pepper, sliced
- 1 carrot, julienned
- 1 cup broccoli florets
- 1 cup snap peas, ends trimmed
- Cooked jasmine rice (for serving)
- Chopped cilantro and crushed peanuts (for garnish)

Instructions:

Prepare Peanut Sauce:
- In a bowl, whisk together peanut butter, soy sauce, honey, rice vinegar, sesame oil, lime juice, minced garlic, grated ginger, and sriracha sauce. If the sauce is too thick, add water gradually to achieve the desired consistency. Set aside.

Stir-Fry Chicken:
- Heat vegetable oil in a wok or large skillet over medium-high heat. Add sliced chicken and stir-fry until it is browned and cooked through.

Add Vegetables:

- Add sliced red and yellow bell peppers, julienned carrot, broccoli florets, and snap peas to the pan. Stir-fry for 3-4 minutes until the vegetables are tender-crisp.

Combine with Peanut Sauce:
- Pour the prepared peanut sauce over the chicken and vegetables. Stir everything well to coat in the sauce.

Finish Stir-Fry:
- Continue to stir-fry for an additional 2-3 minutes until everything is heated through and well-coated.

Serve:
- Serve the Thai Peanut Chicken Stir-Fry over cooked jasmine rice.

Garnish:
- Garnish with chopped cilantro and crushed peanuts on top.

Enjoy:
- Enjoy this Thai Peanut Chicken Stir-Fry as a flavorful and satisfying meal.

Feel free to customize the recipe by adding more vegetables or adjusting the level of spiciness in the peanut sauce. This stir-fry brings together the rich flavors of peanut, soy, and sesame with the freshness of colorful vegetables and tender chicken.

Honey Sesame Shrimp Stir-Fry

Ingredients:

For the Honey Sesame Sauce:

- 1/4 cup soy sauce
- 2 tablespoons honey
- 1 tablespoon rice vinegar
- 1 tablespoon sesame oil
- 1 tablespoon cornstarch
- 1 teaspoon grated ginger
- 2 cloves garlic, minced
- 1 tablespoon sesame seeds

For the Stir-Fry:

- 1 lb (450g) large shrimp, peeled and deveined
- 2 tablespoons vegetable oil
- 1 red bell pepper, sliced
- 1 yellow bell pepper, sliced
- 1 cup snow peas, ends trimmed
- 1 carrot, julienned
- Cooked jasmine rice (for serving)
- Sliced green onions and additional sesame seeds (for garnish)

Instructions:

Prepare Honey Sesame Sauce:
- In a bowl, whisk together soy sauce, honey, rice vinegar, sesame oil, cornstarch, grated ginger, minced garlic, and sesame seeds. Set aside.

Stir-Fry Shrimp:
- Heat vegetable oil in a wok or large skillet over medium-high heat. Add shrimp and stir-fry until they turn pink and opaque. Remove shrimp from the pan and set aside.

Stir-Fry Vegetables:
- In the same pan, add a bit more oil if needed. Add sliced red and yellow bell peppers, snow peas, and julienned carrot. Stir-fry for 3-4 minutes until the vegetables are tender-crisp.

Combine with Honey Sesame Sauce:

- Return the cooked shrimp to the pan with the stir-fried vegetables. Pour the prepared honey sesame sauce over the shrimp and vegetables. Stir everything well to coat in the sauce.

Finish Stir-Fry:
- Continue to stir-fry for an additional 2-3 minutes until everything is heated through and well-coated.

Serve:
- Serve the Honey Sesame Shrimp Stir-Fry over cooked jasmine rice.

Garnish:
- Garnish with sliced green onions and additional sesame seeds on top.

Enjoy:
- Enjoy this Honey Sesame Shrimp Stir-Fry as a sweet and savory delight.

Feel free to customize the recipe by adding more vegetables or adjusting the sweetness and saltiness of the sauce according to your taste preferences. This stir-fry is a perfect combination of succulent shrimp, crisp vegetables, and a flavorful honey sesame glaze.

Broccoli and Tofu in Garlic Sauce Stir-Fry

Ingredients:

For the Garlic Sauce:

- 1/4 cup soy sauce
- 2 tablespoons rice vinegar
- 1 tablespoon sesame oil
- 1 tablespoon hoisin sauce
- 1 tablespoon cornstarch
- 1 tablespoon brown sugar
- 1 tablespoon vegetable broth or water
- 3 cloves garlic, minced
- 1 teaspoon grated ginger

For the Stir-Fry:

- 1 lb (450g) firm tofu, pressed and cubed
- 2 tablespoons vegetable oil
- 1 broccoli crown, cut into florets
- 1 red bell pepper, sliced
- 1 carrot, julienned
- 1 cup snap peas, ends trimmed
- Cooked brown rice or noodles (for serving)
- Sesame seeds and sliced green onions (for garnish)

Instructions:

Prepare Garlic Sauce:
- In a bowl, whisk together soy sauce, rice vinegar, sesame oil, hoisin sauce, cornstarch, brown sugar, vegetable broth (or water), minced garlic, and grated ginger. Set aside.

Stir-Fry Tofu:
- Heat vegetable oil in a wok or large skillet over medium-high heat. Add cubed tofu and stir-fry until it is golden brown on all sides. Remove tofu from the pan and set aside.

Stir-Fry Vegetables:
- In the same pan, add a bit more oil if needed. Add broccoli florets, sliced red bell pepper, julienned carrot, and snap peas. Stir-fry for 3-4 minutes until the vegetables are tender-crisp.

Combine with Garlic Sauce:
- Return the cooked tofu to the pan with the stir-fried vegetables. Pour the prepared garlic sauce over the tofu and vegetables. Stir everything well to coat in the sauce.

Finish Stir-Fry:
- Continue to stir-fry for an additional 2-3 minutes until everything is heated through and well-coated.

Serve:
- Serve the Broccoli and Tofu in Garlic Sauce Stir-Fry over cooked brown rice or noodles.

Garnish:
- Garnish with sesame seeds and sliced green onions on top.

Enjoy:
- Enjoy this Broccoli and Tofu in Garlic Sauce Stir-Fry as a wholesome and flavorful vegetarian meal.

Feel free to customize the recipe by adding other vegetables or adjusting the level of spice in the sauce. This stir-fry offers a perfect balance of textures and flavors with the crispness of vegetables, the firmness of tofu, and the aromatic garlic sauce.

General Tso's Cauliflower Stir-Fry

Ingredients:

For the Cauliflower:

- 1 medium-sized cauliflower, cut into florets
- 1 cup all-purpose flour
- 1 cup water
- 1 teaspoon garlic powder
- Salt and pepper to taste
- Vegetable oil for frying

For the General Tso's Sauce:

- 1/4 cup soy sauce
- 2 tablespoons rice vinegar
- 2 tablespoons hoisin sauce
- 2 tablespoons ketchup
- 2 tablespoons sugar
- 1 tablespoon sesame oil
- 1 tablespoon cornstarch
- 1 teaspoon grated ginger
- 2 cloves garlic, minced
- 1/2 teaspoon red pepper flakes (adjust to taste)

For Stir-Frying:

- 2 tablespoons vegetable oil
- 1 bell pepper, sliced
- 1 green onion, sliced (for garnish)
- Sesame seeds (for garnish)

Instructions:

Prepare Cauliflower:
- In a bowl, whisk together flour, water, garlic powder, salt, and pepper to create a batter. Dip cauliflower florets into the batter, ensuring they are well-coated.
- Heat vegetable oil in a pan for frying. Fry the battered cauliflower until golden brown and crispy. Place on a paper towel to absorb excess oil.

Make General Tso's Sauce:

- In a small bowl, whisk together soy sauce, rice vinegar, hoisin sauce, ketchup, sugar, sesame oil, cornstarch, grated ginger, minced garlic, and red pepper flakes.

Stir-Fry Vegetables:
- In a wok or large skillet, heat 2 tablespoons of vegetable oil. Add sliced bell pepper and stir-fry for 2-3 minutes until slightly softened.

Combine with Sauce:
- Pour the General Tso's sauce over the stir-fried bell pepper. Stir well to coat.

Add Fried Cauliflower:
- Add the crispy cauliflower to the wok. Gently toss everything together until the cauliflower is evenly coated with the sauce.

Finish Stir-Fry:
- Stir-fry for an additional 2-3 minutes until everything is heated through, and the sauce has thickened.

Serve:
- Serve the General Tso's Cauliflower Stir-Fry over steamed rice.

Garnish:
- Garnish with sliced green onions and sesame seeds on top.

Enjoy:
- Enjoy this General Tso's Cauliflower Stir-Fry as a flavorful and satisfying vegetarian dish.

Feel free to adjust the spice level by adding more or less red pepper flakes according to your preference. This dish offers a delightful combination of crispy cauliflower and a rich, savory sauce.

Sriracha Lime Chicken Stir-Fry

Ingredients:

For the Marinade:

- 1 pound boneless, skinless chicken breasts or thighs, thinly sliced
- 3 tablespoons soy sauce
- 2 tablespoons sriracha sauce
- 2 tablespoons honey
- 2 tablespoons fresh lime juice
- 2 cloves garlic, minced
- 1 teaspoon grated ginger
- 1 tablespoon vegetable oil

For the Stir-Fry:

- 2 tablespoons vegetable oil
- 1 onion, thinly sliced
- 1 bell pepper, thinly sliced (any color)
- 1 carrot, julienned
- 1 cup snap peas or snow peas, ends trimmed
- 1 cup broccoli florets
- Cooked rice or noodles for serving
- Sesame seeds and chopped cilantro for garnish (optional)

Instructions:

Marinate the Chicken:
- In a bowl, whisk together soy sauce, sriracha sauce, honey, lime juice, minced garlic, grated ginger, and vegetable oil to create the marinade.
- Add sliced chicken to the marinade, ensuring all pieces are well coated. Let it marinate for at least 15-30 minutes, or you can refrigerate it for a few hours for more flavor.

Stir-Fry the Chicken:
- Heat 2 tablespoons of vegetable oil in a large wok or skillet over medium-high heat.

- Add the marinated chicken to the wok and stir-fry until the chicken is fully cooked and browned. This should take about 5-7 minutes.

Cook Vegetables:
- Push the cooked chicken to one side of the wok and add a bit more oil if needed.
- Add sliced onion, bell pepper, julienned carrot, snap peas, and broccoli florets to the wok. Stir-fry the vegetables for 3-5 minutes until they are tender-crisp.

Combine Chicken and Vegetables:
- Once the vegetables are cooked, combine them with the cooked chicken in the wok. Toss everything together to ensure an even distribution of flavors.

Serve:
- Serve the Sriracha Lime Chicken Stir-Fry over cooked rice or noodles.

Garnish (Optional):
- Garnish with sesame seeds and chopped cilantro for added flavor and presentation.

Adjust the sriracha amount based on your spice preference. This stir-fry offers a perfect balance of heat and citrusy zing. Enjoy your Sriracha Lime Chicken Stir-Fry!

Honey Ginger Salmon Stir-Fry

Ingredients:

For the Salmon Marinade:

- 1 pound salmon fillets, cut into bite-sized pieces
- 3 tablespoons soy sauce
- 2 tablespoons honey
- 1 tablespoon fresh ginger, grated
- 2 cloves garlic, minced
- 1 tablespoon sesame oil

For the Stir-Fry:

- 2 tablespoons vegetable oil
- 1 onion, thinly sliced
- 1 bell pepper, thinly sliced (any color)
- 1 carrot, julienned
- 1 cup broccoli florets
- 1 cup snap peas or snow peas, ends trimmed
- Cooked rice or noodles for serving
- Sesame seeds and chopped green onions for garnish (optional)

Instructions:

Marinate the Salmon:
- In a bowl, mix together soy sauce, honey, grated ginger, minced garlic, and sesame oil to create the marinade.
- Place the salmon pieces in the marinade, ensuring they are well coated. Let it marinate for at least 15-30 minutes.

Stir-Fry the Salmon:
- Heat 2 tablespoons of vegetable oil in a large wok or skillet over medium-high heat.
- Add the marinated salmon pieces to the wok and cook until the salmon is browned and cooked through. This should take about 4-6 minutes.

Cook Vegetables:

- Push the cooked salmon to one side of the wok and add a bit more oil if needed.
- Add sliced onion, bell pepper, julienned carrot, broccoli florets, and snap peas to the wok. Stir-fry the vegetables for 3-5 minutes until they are tender-crisp.

Combine Salmon and Vegetables:
- Once the vegetables are cooked, combine them with the cooked salmon in the wok. Toss everything together to ensure an even distribution of flavors.

Serve:
- Serve the Honey Ginger Salmon Stir-Fry over cooked rice or noodles.

Garnish (Optional):
- Garnish with sesame seeds and chopped green onions for added flavor and presentation.

This Honey Ginger Salmon Stir-Fry provides a perfect balance of sweetness from honey, the warmth of ginger, and the savory goodness of soy sauce. Enjoy your delicious and healthy stir-fry!

Teriyaki Vegetable Stir-Fry

Ingredients:

For the Teriyaki Sauce:

- 1/4 cup soy sauce
- 2 tablespoons mirin (sweet rice wine)
- 2 tablespoons sake (or dry white wine)
- 2 tablespoons brown sugar
- 1 teaspoon sesame oil
- 1 teaspoon grated ginger
- 2 cloves garlic, minced
- 1 tablespoon cornstarch mixed with 2 tablespoons water (optional, for thickening)

For the Stir-Fry:

- 2 tablespoons vegetable oil
- 1 onion, sliced
- 2 bell peppers, sliced (different colors for visual appeal)
- 1 carrot, julienned
- 1 zucchini, sliced
- 1 cup broccoli florets
- 1 cup snap peas or snow peas, ends trimmed
- 1 cup sliced mushrooms
- 1 cup firm tofu, pressed and cubed (optional)
- Cooked rice or noodles for serving

Instructions:

Prepare the Teriyaki Sauce:
- In a small bowl, whisk together soy sauce, mirin, sake, brown sugar, sesame oil, grated ginger, and minced garlic.
- If you prefer a thicker sauce, mix the cornstarch with water to create a slurry. Stir it into the sauce mixture. Set aside.

Stir-Fry the Vegetables:

- Heat vegetable oil in a large wok or skillet over medium-high heat.
- Add sliced onion and stir-fry for 1-2 minutes until slightly softened.

Add Vegetables:
- Add bell peppers, julienned carrot, sliced zucchini, broccoli florets, snap peas, and mushrooms to the wok.
- Stir-fry the vegetables for about 5-7 minutes until they are tender-crisp. Adjust the cooking time based on your preference for the crunchiness of the vegetables.

Add Tofu (Optional):
- If using tofu, add the cubed tofu to the wok and gently stir to combine with the vegetables. Cook for an additional 2-3 minutes.

Add Teriyaki Sauce:
- Pour the prepared teriyaki sauce over the vegetables and tofu. Toss everything together to ensure even coating.

Serve:
- Remove the wok from heat and serve the Teriyaki Vegetable Stir-Fry over cooked rice or noodles.

Garnish (Optional):
- Garnish with sesame seeds, chopped green onions, or cilantro for added flavor and presentation.

Enjoy your delicious Teriyaki Vegetable Stir-Fry! Feel free to customize the vegetables based on your preferences.

Spicy Basil Shrimp Stir-Fry

Ingredients:

For the Stir-Fry Sauce:

- 3 tablespoons soy sauce
- 1 tablespoon oyster sauce
- 1 tablespoon fish sauce
- 1 tablespoon hoisin sauce
- 1 tablespoon rice vinegar
- 1 tablespoon brown sugar
- 1 tablespoon Sriracha sauce (adjust for spice level)
- 1 tablespoon vegetable oil

For the Stir-Fry:

- 1 pound large shrimp, peeled and deveined
- 2 tablespoons vegetable oil
- 4 cloves garlic, minced
- 1 red chili, thinly sliced (adjust for spice level)
- 1 bell pepper, thinly sliced
- 1 cup snap peas or snow peas, ends trimmed
- 1 cup fresh basil leaves, preferably Thai basil
- Cooked rice for serving

Instructions:

Prepare the Stir-Fry Sauce:
- In a small bowl, whisk together soy sauce, oyster sauce, fish sauce, hoisin sauce, rice vinegar, brown sugar, Sriracha sauce, and vegetable oil. Set aside.

Cook the Shrimp:
- Heat 2 tablespoons of vegetable oil in a large wok or skillet over medium-high heat.
- Add minced garlic and sliced red chili to the wok, stir-frying for about 30 seconds until fragrant.
- Add the shrimp to the wok and stir-fry until they turn pink and opaque, approximately 2-3 minutes.

Add Vegetables:
- Add sliced bell pepper and snap peas to the wok. Stir-fry for an additional 2-3 minutes until the vegetables are tender-crisp.

Add Stir-Fry Sauce:
- Pour the prepared stir-fry sauce over the shrimp and vegetables. Toss everything together to coat evenly and let it simmer for 1-2 minutes.

Add Basil:
- Add fresh basil leaves to the wok and toss until the basil wilts and releases its aroma.

Serve:
- Remove the wok from heat and serve the Spicy Basil Shrimp Stir-Fry over cooked rice.

Garnish (Optional):
- Garnish with additional fresh basil leaves, sliced red chili, or chopped green onions for added flavor and presentation.

Enjoy your Spicy Basil Shrimp Stir-Fry! Adjust the level of spice according to your preference, and feel free to customize the vegetables to suit your taste.

Orange Glazed Tofu Stir-Fry

Ingredients:

For the Orange Glaze:

- 1/2 cup orange juice (freshly squeezed is preferable)
- 2 tablespoons soy sauce
- 2 tablespoons rice vinegar
- 2 tablespoons maple syrup or honey
- 1 tablespoon cornstarch

For the Stir-Fry:

- 1 block (about 14 oz) firm or extra-firm tofu, pressed and cubed
- 2 tablespoons vegetable oil
- 1 bell pepper, thinly sliced (any color)
- 1 carrot, julienned
- 1 cup broccoli florets
- 1 cup snap peas or snow peas, ends trimmed
- 2 cloves garlic, minced
- 1 tablespoon fresh ginger, grated
- Cooked rice or noodles for serving
- Sesame seeds and sliced green onions for garnish (optional)

Instructions:

Prepare the Orange Glaze:
- In a small bowl, whisk together orange juice, soy sauce, rice vinegar, maple syrup (or honey), and cornstarch until well combined. Set aside.

Prepare the Tofu:
- Press the tofu to remove excess water, and then cut it into cubes.

Stir-Fry the Tofu:
- Heat 1 tablespoon of vegetable oil in a large skillet or wok over medium-high heat.
- Add the tofu cubes and cook until they are golden brown on all sides. This should take about 8-10 minutes. Once done, remove the tofu from the skillet and set it aside.

Cook Vegetables:

- In the same skillet, add another tablespoon of oil if needed.
- Add sliced bell pepper, julienned carrot, broccoli florets, snap peas, minced garlic, and grated ginger to the skillet. Stir-fry for about 5-7 minutes until the vegetables are tender-crisp.

Combine Tofu and Vegetables:
- Return the cooked tofu to the skillet with the vegetables.

Add Orange Glaze:
- Pour the prepared orange glaze over the tofu and vegetables. Toss everything together to coat evenly. Allow it to simmer for 2-3 minutes until the sauce thickens.

Serve:
- Serve the Orange Glazed Tofu Stir-Fry over cooked rice or noodles.

Garnish (Optional):
- Garnish with sesame seeds and sliced green onions for added flavor and presentation.

Enjoy your delicious and flavorful Orange Glazed Tofu Stir-Fry! Adjust the sweetness or tanginess according to your taste preferences.

Mongolian Tofu Stir-Fry

Ingredients:

For the Tofu:

- 1 block (about 14 oz) firm or extra-firm tofu, pressed and cubed
- 3 tablespoons soy sauce
- 2 tablespoons cornstarch
- 2 tablespoons vegetable oil

For the Stir-Fry Sauce:

- 1/4 cup soy sauce
- 2 tablespoons hoisin sauce
- 2 tablespoons rice vinegar
- 2 tablespoons brown sugar
- 1 teaspoon sesame oil

For the Stir-Fry:

- 1 tablespoon vegetable oil
- 1 onion, thinly sliced
- 2 cloves garlic, minced
- 1 tablespoon fresh ginger, grated
- 1 bell pepper, thinly sliced (any color)
- 1 carrot, julienned
- 3 green onions, sliced (white and green parts separated)
- Sesame seeds for garnish (optional)

Instructions:

Prepare the Tofu:
- In a bowl, combine cubed tofu with 3 tablespoons of soy sauce. Let it marinate for at least 15 minutes.
- Coat the marinated tofu in cornstarch, shaking off any excess.

Cook the Tofu:

- Heat 2 tablespoons of vegetable oil in a large skillet or wok over medium-high heat.
- Add the tofu cubes and cook until they are golden brown and crispy on all sides. Once done, remove the tofu from the skillet and set it aside.

Prepare the Stir-Fry Sauce:
- In a bowl, whisk together 1/4 cup soy sauce, hoisin sauce, rice vinegar, brown sugar, and sesame oil. Set aside.

Cook Vegetables:
- In the same skillet, add 1 tablespoon of vegetable oil if needed.
- Add sliced onion, minced garlic, and grated ginger to the skillet. Stir-fry for about 1-2 minutes until fragrant.

Add Vegetables:
- Add sliced bell pepper, julienned carrot, and the white parts of the green onions to the skillet. Stir-fry for an additional 3-4 minutes until the vegetables are tender-crisp.

Combine Tofu and Vegetables:
- Return the cooked tofu to the skillet with the vegetables.

Add Stir-Fry Sauce:
- Pour the prepared stir-fry sauce over the tofu and vegetables. Toss everything together to coat evenly. Allow it to simmer for 2-3 minutes until the sauce thickens.

Serve:
- Serve the Mongolian Tofu Stir-Fry over cooked rice.

Garnish (Optional):
- Garnish with the green parts of the sliced green onions and sesame seeds for added flavor and presentation.

Enjoy your delicious Mongolian Tofu Stir-Fry! Adjust the sauce ingredients according to your taste preferences.

Soy Chili Beef and Noodle Stir-Fry

Ingredients:

For the Sauce:

- 1/4 cup soy sauce
- 2 tablespoons oyster sauce
- 2 tablespoons hoisin sauce
- 1 tablespoon chili garlic sauce (adjust for spice level)
- 1 tablespoon brown sugar
- 1 tablespoon rice vinegar
- 1 teaspoon sesame oil

For the Stir-Fry:

- 8 oz (about 225g) flank steak or sirloin, thinly sliced
- 8 oz (about 225g) wide rice noodles, cooked according to package instructions
- 2 tablespoons vegetable oil
- 1 onion, thinly sliced
- 1 bell pepper, thinly sliced (any color)
- 2 carrots, julienned
- 3 cloves garlic, minced
- 1 tablespoon fresh ginger, grated
- 2 green onions, sliced (white and green parts separated)
- Sesame seeds for garnish (optional)

Instructions:

Prepare the Sauce:
- In a bowl, whisk together soy sauce, oyster sauce, hoisin sauce, chili garlic sauce, brown sugar, rice vinegar, and sesame oil. Set aside.

Stir-Fry the Beef:
- Heat 1 tablespoon of vegetable oil in a large skillet or wok over medium-high heat.
- Add the thinly sliced beef and stir-fry until it's browned and cooked through. Once done, remove the beef from the skillet and set it aside.

Cook the Vegetables:
- In the same skillet, add another tablespoon of oil if needed.
- Add sliced onion, bell pepper, julienned carrots, minced garlic, and grated ginger to the skillet. Stir-fry for about 3-4 minutes until the vegetables are tender-crisp.

Combine Beef and Vegetables:
- Return the cooked beef to the skillet with the vegetables.

Add Sauce and Noodles:
- Pour the prepared sauce over the beef and vegetables. Toss everything together to coat evenly.
- Add the cooked rice noodles to the skillet and toss until well combined.

Finish and Serve:
- Allow the stir-fry to heat through for an additional 2-3 minutes.
- Garnish with sliced green onions and sesame seeds if desired.

Serve:
- Serve the Soy Chili Beef and Noodle Stir-Fry immediately, and enjoy!

Adjust the chili garlic sauce according to your spice preference. This stir-fry offers a perfect balance of savory, sweet, and spicy flavors.

Lemon Herb Chicken Stir-Fry

Ingredients:

For the Chicken Marinade:

- 1 pound boneless, skinless chicken breasts or thighs, thinly sliced
- 2 tablespoons olive oil
- Zest and juice of 1 lemon
- 2 cloves garlic, minced
- 1 teaspoon dried oregano
- 1 teaspoon dried thyme
- Salt and pepper to taste

For the Stir-Fry:

- 2 tablespoons olive oil
- 1 onion, thinly sliced
- 1 bell pepper, thinly sliced (any color)
- 1 zucchini, thinly sliced
- 1 cup cherry tomatoes, halved
- 2 tablespoons fresh basil, chopped
- 2 tablespoons fresh parsley, chopped
- Cooked quinoa or rice for serving

Instructions:

Marinate the Chicken:
- In a bowl, mix together olive oil, lemon zest, lemon juice, minced garlic, dried oregano, dried thyme, salt, and pepper.
- Add the thinly sliced chicken to the marinade, ensuring it is well-coated. Let it marinate for at least 15-30 minutes.

Stir-Fry the Chicken:
- Heat 2 tablespoons of olive oil in a large skillet or wok over medium-high heat.
- Add the marinated chicken to the skillet and stir-fry until it is fully cooked and browned. This should take about 5-7 minutes.

Cook Vegetables:
- Push the cooked chicken to one side of the skillet and add a bit more oil if needed.
- Add sliced onion, bell pepper, zucchini, and cherry tomatoes to the skillet. Stir-fry the vegetables for 3-5 minutes until they are tender-crisp.

Combine Chicken and Vegetables:
- Once the vegetables are cooked, combine them with the cooked chicken in the skillet. Toss everything together to ensure an even distribution of flavors.

Add Fresh Herbs:
- Stir in fresh basil and parsley, mixing well to incorporate the herbs into the stir-fry.

Serve:
- Remove the skillet from heat and serve the Lemon Herb Chicken Stir-Fry over cooked quinoa or rice.

Garnish (Optional):
- Garnish with additional fresh herbs or a slice of lemon for added flavor and presentation.

Enjoy your delightful Lemon Herb Chicken Stir-Fry! Adjust the herbs and lemon to suit your taste preferences.

Hoisin Eggplant and Tofu Stir-Fry

Ingredients:

For the Sauce:

- 1/4 cup hoisin sauce
- 2 tablespoons soy sauce
- 1 tablespoon rice vinegar
- 1 tablespoon maple syrup or brown sugar
- 1 tablespoon sesame oil
- 1 tablespoon cornstarch mixed with 2 tablespoons water (optional, for thickening)

For the Stir-Fry:

- 1 medium-sized eggplant, cut into bite-sized cubes
- 1 block (about 14 oz) firm tofu, pressed and cubed
- 3 tablespoons vegetable oil, divided
- 3 cloves garlic, minced
- 1 tablespoon fresh ginger, grated
- 1 red bell pepper, thinly sliced
- 2 green onions, sliced (white and green parts separated)
- Cooked rice or noodles for serving
- Sesame seeds for garnish (optional)

Instructions:

Prepare the Sauce:
- In a bowl, whisk together hoisin sauce, soy sauce, rice vinegar, maple syrup (or brown sugar), sesame oil, and, if desired, the cornstarch-water mixture. Set aside.

Cook the Tofu:
- Heat 2 tablespoons of vegetable oil in a large skillet or wok over medium-high heat.
- Add cubed tofu to the skillet and cook until it's golden brown on all sides. Once done, remove the tofu from the skillet and set it aside.

Stir-Fry the Eggplant:
- In the same skillet, add another tablespoon of oil if needed.
- Add the cubed eggplant and stir-fry until it's tender and golden brown. This might take about 5-7 minutes.

Add Garlic and Ginger:
- Add minced garlic and grated ginger to the skillet with the eggplant. Stir-fry for about 1-2 minutes until fragrant.

Combine Tofu and Vegetables:
- Return the cooked tofu to the skillet with the eggplant.

Add Sauce and Peppers:
- Pour the prepared sauce over the tofu, eggplant, and stir-fry. Add sliced red bell pepper and toss everything together to coat evenly. Allow it to simmer for 2-3 minutes.

Serve:
- Serve the Hoisin Eggplant and Tofu Stir-Fry over cooked rice or noodles.

Garnish (Optional):
- Garnish with sliced green onions and sesame seeds for added flavor and presentation.

Enjoy your delicious Hoisin Eggplant and Tofu Stir-Fry! Adjust the sauce ingredients to suit your taste preferences.

Pineapple Fried Quinoa Stir-Fry

Ingredients:

For the Stir-Fry Sauce:

- 3 tablespoons soy sauce
- 2 tablespoons hoisin sauce
- 1 tablespoon rice vinegar
- 1 tablespoon sesame oil
- 1 tablespoon maple syrup or brown sugar
- 1 teaspoon grated ginger
- 2 cloves garlic, minced

For the Stir-Fry:

- 2 cups cooked quinoa (cooled)
- 1 tablespoon vegetable oil
- 1 onion, finely chopped
- 2 bell peppers, diced (any color)
- 1 cup snap peas or snow peas, ends trimmed
- 1 carrot, julienned
- 1 cup pineapple chunks (fresh or canned)
- 1 cup diced firm tofu or cooked chicken (optional)
- 2 green onions, sliced
- Sesame seeds for garnish (optional)

Instructions:

Prepare the Stir-Fry Sauce:
- In a bowl, whisk together soy sauce, hoisin sauce, rice vinegar, sesame oil, maple syrup (or brown sugar), grated ginger, and minced garlic. Set aside.

Stir-Fry the Vegetables:
- Heat vegetable oil in a large wok or skillet over medium-high heat.
- Add chopped onion, diced bell peppers, snap peas, and julienned carrot. Stir-fry for 3-4 minutes until the vegetables are slightly tender but still crisp.

Add Pineapple and Tofu/Chicken (Optional):
- Add pineapple chunks and tofu or cooked chicken (if using) to the wok. Stir-fry for an additional 2-3 minutes until everything is heated through.

Stir in Quinoa:
- Add the cooked and cooled quinoa to the wok. Stir everything together to combine.

Pour in Stir-Fry Sauce:
- Pour the prepared stir-fry sauce over the quinoa and vegetables. Toss everything together to coat evenly. Cook for an additional 2-3 minutes.

Finish and Garnish:
- Stir in sliced green onions and cook for another minute until they are slightly wilted.
- Optionally, garnish with sesame seeds for added flavor and presentation.

Serve:
- Serve the Pineapple Fried Quinoa Stir-Fry hot as a main dish.

Enjoy your delightful Pineapple Fried Quinoa Stir-Fry! This dish is not only delicious but also packed with a variety of nutrients and flavors.

www.ingramcontent.com/pod-product-compliance
Lightning Source LLC
LaVergne TN
LVHW081601060526
838201LV00054B/2016